365

Historic Houses
and Castles

visit**Britain**™

Information
at your fingertips

When it comes to having a great day out, there's no finer place than England. This pocket guide is brimming with a wide selection of historic houses and castles, each one offering something of special interest to the visitor, from the splendour of Chatsworth House to the otherworldly beauty of Brighton Pavilion. Whether you want to marvel at the architecture, gaze adoringly at the furniture, or enjoy what's on offer in the grounds, there's lots to explore. Dip into this guide and you'll find 365 buildings of historical importance that welcome visitors, one for every day of the year!

The attractions in this guide are alphabetically ordered by county, and then by town. Some attractions will be accompanied by the following symbol:

The Quality Assured Visitor Attraction sign indicates that the attraction is assessed annually and meets the standards required to receive the quality marque.

Key to attraction facilities

☕	Café/restaurant
⛫	Picnic area
🐕	Dogs allowed
🐕‍🦺	No dogs except service dogs
♿	Full disabled access
♿	Partial disabled access

For more information on attractions in England, visit enjoyengland.com.

3

How to use
this guide

Each visitor attraction contains the following
essential information.

① ③ ④ ②

Hardwick Hall   DOE LEA

Hardwick Hall, Doe Lea, S44 5QJ
t: (01246) 850430   **w:** nationaltrust.org.uk

open: Apr–Oct, Wed–Thu, Sat–Sun 1200–1630.
admission: £9.00

description: Elizabethan country
house, gardens
and parkland, with
outstanding collections
of furniture, tapestry and
needlework.

facilities:

⑤ ⑦ ⑥

1   Name
2   City/Town
3   Address and contact details
4   Opening times
5   Price of admission
6   Description
7   Facilities

Admission is free if the price is not specified. The price is based on a
single adult admission.

Please note, as changes often occur after press date, it is advisable
to confirm opening times and admission prices before travelling.

Moggerhanger Park

Moggerhanger Park, Park Road, Moggerhanger, MK44 3RW
t: (01767) 641007   **w:** moggerhangerpark.com

open:	Tea rooms/restaurant: all year 1100–1600. House tours: 16 Jun–9 Sep 1200 & 1430.
admission:	£7.50
description:	Recently restored Grade I Georgian house, as designed by Sir John Soane. Guided tours daily throughout the summer; free access to woodlands and exhibition all year round; conference facilities available. Tea rooms open every day from 1100 to 1600.
facilities:	☕ 🚶 ♿

Woburn Abbey

Woburn Abbey, Woburn, MK17 9WA
t: (01525) 290666   **w:** discoverwoburn.co.uk

open:	Apr–Sep, daily 1100–1600.
admission:	£10.50
description:	An 18thC Palladian mansion, altered by Henry Holland, the Prince Regent's architect, containing a collection of English silver, French and English furniture and art.
facilities:	☕ 🚶 ⛱ ♿

Basildon Park

Basildon Park, Lower Basildon, RG8 9NR
t: (0118) 984 3040   **w:** nationaltrust.org.uk

open:	House: Apr–Oct, Wed–Sun 1200–1700. Grounds: Apr–Oct, Wed–Sun 1100–1700.
admission:	£6.00

description: A classical 18thC house by John Carr of York, with an unusual octagon room, fine plasterwork and the decorative shell room. Situated in 400 acres of parkland and woodland.

facilities: ⬛ 🐕 ⛉ ♿

Windsor Castle

Windsor Castle, Windsor, SL4 1NJ
t: (020) 7766 7304   **w:** royalcollection.org.uk

open:	Apr–Oct, daily 0945–1715. Nov–Feb, daily 0945–1615.
admission:	£14.20

description: The oldest and largest occupied castle in the world and Official residence of HM The Queen and royal residence for nine centuries. State apartments, Queen Mary's Doll's House.

facilities: 🏹 ♿

Waddesdon Manor
AYLESBURY

Waddesdon Manor, Waddesdon, Aylesbury,
HP18 0JH   **t:** (01296) 653226   **w:** waddesdon.org.uk

open: Gardens: Apr–Dec,
Wed–Sun, Bank Hols 1000–1700.
House: Apr–Oct, Wed–Fri,
Bank Hols 1200–1600, Sat–Sun
1100–1600.
admission: £15.00

description: A French Renaissance-style chateau housing
the Rothschild Collection of art treasures, wine
cellars, two licensed restaurants, gift and wine
shops, an aviary and spectacular gardens.

facilities:

Hughenden Manor
HIGH WYCOMBE

Hughenden Manor, High Wycombe, HP14 4LA
t: (01494) 755573   **w:** nationaltrust.org.uk

open: House: Apr–Oct, Wed–Sun 1300–1700. Dec,
Sat–Sun 1200–1500. Garden: Apr–Oct, Wed–
Sun 1100–1700. Dec, Sat–Sun 1100–1600.
Park: Daily.
admission: £6.40

description: Victorian home of Prime Minister and
statesman Benjamin Disraeli from 1848 until
his death in 1881. Most of his furniture, books
and pictures remain in this, his private retreat.

facilities:

Claydon House

Claydon House, Middle Claydon, MK18 2EY
t: (01296) 730349   **w:** nationaltrust.org.uk

open:	Apr–Oct, Mon–Wed, Sat–Sun 1300–1700.
admission:	£5.50

description: An 18thC house containing a series of magnificent and unique rococo staterooms with important carvings. Museums of Florence Nightingale and the Crimean War.

facilities: ☕ ✗ ♿

Bletchley Park

Bletchley Park, The Mansion, Bletchley Park, Milton Keynes, MK3 6EB   **t:** (01908) 640404   **w:** bletchleypark.org.uk

open:	Apr–Oct, Mon–Fri 0930–1700, Sat–Sun 1030–1700. Nov–Mar Mon–Sun 1030–1600.
admission:	£10.00

description: Victorian mansion and wartime buildings with exhibitions of wartime code-breaking including the famous Enigma machines. Also featuring Churchill memorabilia, the Home Front exhibition, and many more attractions throughout the park.

facilities: ☕ ♿ 🪑 ♿

Cliveden

Cliveden, Taplow, SL6 0JA
t: (01628) 605069   **w:** nationaltrust.org.uk

open: House: Apr–Oct, Thu, Sun 1500–1730. Garden: Apr–Oct, daily 1100–1800. Nov–Dec, daily 1100–1600. Woodland: Apr–Oct, daily 1100–1730. Nov–Feb, daily 1100–1600.

admission: £7.50

description: Overlooking the Thames, the present house, built in 1851, was once the home of Lady Astor, and is situated in 375 acres of gardens, woodland and riverside walks.

facilities: ▭ ⼓ ⌗

Taplow Court

Taplow Court, Berry Hill, Taplow, SL6 0ER
t: (01628) 591215

open: May–Jul, Sun, Bank Hols 1400–1700.

description: Set high above the Thames, affording spectacular views, Taplow Court was remodelled in the mid-19thC by William Burn. Tranquil gardens and grounds. Anglo-Saxon burial mound. Temporary exhibitions.

facilities: ▭ ⼓ ⼌ ⌗

West Wycombe Park

West Wycombe Park, West Wycombe, HP14 3AJ
t: (01494) 513569   w: nationaltrust.org.uk

open:	Grounds: Apr–Aug, Mon–Thu, Sun 1400–1800. House: Jun–Aug, Mon–Thu, Sun 1400–1800.
admission:	£6.00
description:	Palladian house with frescoes and painted ceilings fashioned for Sir Francis Dashwood in the mid 18thC. Landscape and lake also laid out at the same time.
facilities:	⚡ ♿

Wimpole Hall and Home Farm: The National Trust

Wimpole Hall and Home Farm: The National Trust,
Arrington, SG8 0BW   t: (01223) 206000
w: nationaltrust.org.uk

open:	Apr–Jul, Mon–Wed, Sat–Sun 1030–1700. Aug, Mon–Thu, Sat–Sun 1030–1700. Sep–Oct, Mon–Wed, Sat–Sun 1030–1700. Nov–Feb, Sat–Sun 1100–1600.
admission:	£6.60
description:	An 18thC house in a landscaped park with a folly, Chinese bridge, plunge bath and yellow drawing room in the house, the work of John Soane. Home Farm is a rare breeds centre.
facilities:	🍴 ⚡ 🪑 ♿

Elton Hall

Elton Hall, Elton, PE8 6SH
t: (01832) 280468   **w:** eltonhall.com

open: Jun, Wed, 1400–1700. Jul–Aug, Wed, Thu, Sun 1400–1700.

admission: £7.50

description: A historic house and gardens open to the public with a fine collection of paintings, furniture, books and Henry VIII's prayer book. There is also a restored rose garden.

facilities: ⚔ ♿

Anglesey Abbey, Gardens and Lode Mill

Anglesey Abbey, Gardens and Lode Mill, Quy Road, Lode, CB25 9EJ   **t:** (01223) 810080   **w:** nationaltrust.org.uk

open: Abbey: Apr–Oct, Wed–Sun 1300–1700. Gardens: Apr–Oct, Wed–Sun 1030–1730. Lode Mill: Apr–Oct, Wed–Sun 1300–1700.

admission: £8.80

description: A 13thC abbey with a later Jacobean-style house and the famous Fairhaven collection of paintings and furniture. There is also an outstanding 100-acre garden and arboretum.

facilities: 🍽 ⚔ ⛱ ♿

Peckover House and Gardens

Peckover House and Gardens, North Brink, Wisbech, PE13 1JR   **t:** (01945) 583463   **w:** nationaltrust.org.uk

open:	House: Apr–Oct, Mon–Wed, Sat–Sun 1300–1630. Garden: Apr–Oct, Mon–Wed, Sat–Sun 1200–1700.
admission:	£5.00
description:	A merchant's house on the north brink of the River Nene, built in 1722 with a plaster and wood rococo interior and a notable and rare Victorian garden with unusual trees.
facilities:	🍽 🍴

Beeston Castle (English Heritage)

Beeston Castle (English Heritage), Chapel Lane, Beeston, CW6 9TX   **t:** (01829) 260464
w: english-heritage.org.uk

open:	See website for details.
admission:	£4.00
description:	A ruined 13thC castle situated on top of the Peckforton Hills, with views of the surrounding countryside. Exhibitions are also held featuring the castle's history.

facilities: 🍴 ⛱ ♿

Stanley Palace

Stanley Palace, Watergate Street, Chester, CH1 2LF
t: (01244) 325586 **w:** stanleypalace.com

open:	All year, Tue–Fri 1000–1300, 1400–1600.
description:	A late-16thC town house with original beams and floors, 18thC panelling and a plaster ceiling. The house contains period furniture of historical interest.
facilities:	夨 ᵭ

Little Moreton Hall (NT)

Little Moreton Hall (National Trust), Congleton, CW12 4SD
t: (01260) 272018 **w:** nationaltrust.org.uk

open:	Mar, Wed–Sun 1130–1600. Apr–Oct, Wed–Sun, 1130–1700. Nov, Sat–Sun 1130–1600.
admission:	£5.50
description:	A perfect example of a half-timbered moated manor house with Great Hall, Elizabethan long gallery and chapel. Elizabethan-style knot and herb garden.
facilities:	⬛ 夨 ⧓ ᵭ

DISLEY

Lyme Park (NT)

Lyme Park (National Trust), Disley, SK12 2NX
t: (01663) 762023 **w:** nationaltrust.org.uk

open: House: Apr–Oct, Mon–Tue, Fri–Sun 1300–1700. Park: Apr–Sep, daily 0800–2030. Oct–Feb, daily 0800–1800.
admission: £6.50

description: A National Trust country estate set in 1,377 acres of moorland, woodland and park. The magnificent house has 17 acres of historic gardens.

facilities: ☕ 🐕 ⛺ ♿

KNUTSFORD

Tabley House Stately Home

Tabley House Stately Home, Tabley House, Tabley Lane, Knutsford, WA16 0HB **t:** (01565) 750151
w: tableyhouse.co.uk

open: Apr–Oct, Thu–Sun, Bank Hols 1400–1700.
admission: £4.00

description: A fine Palladian house designed by John Carr in 1761, containing a collection of English paintings, period furniture and Leicester family memorabilia.

facilities: ☕ 🐕 ⛺ ♿

Adlington Hall

MACCLESFIELD

Adlington Hall, Mill Lane, Macclesfield, SK10 4LF
t: (01625) 829206   **w:** adlingtonhall.com

open:	Aug, Mon–Wed, Sun 1400–1700.
admission:	£6.00

description: The home of the Legh family since 1315, Adlington Hall combines a medieval Hall with Cheshire black-and-white and elegant Georgian additions.

facilities:

Dorfold Hall

NANTWICH

Dorfold Hall, Nantwich, CW5 8LD
t: (01270) 625245

open:	Apr–Oct, Wed, Bank Hols 1400–1700.
admission:	£5.00

description: A Jacobean house built in 1616, with beautifully plastered ceilings, oak panelling and a woodland garden.

facilities:

Arley Hall & Gardens

Arley Hall & Gardens, Northwich, CW9 6NA
t: (01565) 777353   **w:** arleyhallandgardens.com

open:	31 Mar–30 Sep 1100–1700. Hall open Tue, Sun and Bank Holidays only.
admission:	£5.00

description: Rich in history and beauty, Arley offers award-winning gardens and a beautiful Victorian/Jacobean Hall. Marvel at the double herbaceous border, giant Ilex columns and explore the Victorian Rooftree and delightful woodland trails in the Grove.

facilities:

Capesthorne Hall

Capesthorne Hall, Siddington, SK11 9JY
t: (01625) 861221   **w:** capesthorne.com

open:	Apr–Oct, Wed, Sun, Bank Hols 1330–1600.
admission:	£4.00

description: Sculptures, paintings, furniture and family monuments. A Georgian chapel, tearooms, gardens, lakes, nature walks and a touring caravan park.

facilities:

Walton Hall and Gardens

Walton Hall and Gardens, Walton Lea Road, Higher Walton,
Warrington, WA4 6SN   **t:** (01925) 261957
w: warrington.gov.uk/waltongardens

open: Daily 0800–dusk.

description: An ideal place for a family day out, with
                   extensive lawns, picnic areas, ornamental
                   gardens, woodland trails and a children's zoo.

facilities: ☕ 🐕 🪑 ♿

Lanhydrock

Lanhydrock, Bodmin, PL30 5AD
t: (01208) 265950   **w:** nationaltrust.org.uk

open: House: Apr–Sep, Tue–Sun 1100–1730. Oct,
                   Tue–Sat 1100–1700. Gardens: Daily 1000–
                   1800.
admission: £9.40

description: A 17thC house largely rebuilt
                   after a fire in 1881. The 116ft
                   gallery with magnificent
                   plaster ceiling illustrates
                   scenes from the Old
                   Testament. Park, gardens, walks.

facilities: ☕ 🍴 🪑 ♿

Godolphin House

Godolphin House, Godolphin Cross, Breage, TR13 9RE
t: (01736) 763194   **w:** godolphinhouse.com

open:	All year, Tue–Fri, Sun, Bank Hols 1100–1700.
admission:	£6.00

description:	Privately owned mansion (c1475) complete with side garden and stables. Unique architectural features survive. Beautiful surroundings.

facilities: ☕ 🚶 ♿

Mount Edgcumbe House and Park

Mount Edgcumbe House and Park, Cremyll, PL10 1HZ
t: (01752) 822236   **w:** mountedgcumbe.gov.uk

open:	Apr–Sep, Mon–Thu, Sun 1100–1630.
admission:	£4.50

description: Restored Tudor mansion, past home of Earl of Mount Edgcumbe. French, Italian and English formal gardens with temples and 800 acres of parkland.

facilities: ☕ 🚶 ⛱ ♿

Pendennis Castle

Pendennis Castle, Falmouth, TR11 4LP
t: (01326) 316594   **w:** english-heritage.org.uk/pendennis

open: Apr–Jun, Sep, Mon–Fri, Sun 1000–1700, Sat 1000–1600. Jul–Aug, Mon–Fri, Sun 1000–1800, Sat 1000–1600. Oct–Mar, daily 1000–1600.
admission: £5.40

description: Guards the entrance to the Fal estuary, along with its sister castle, St Mawes. Well-preserved coastal fort built by Henry VIII c1540.

facilities:

Restormel Castle

Restormel Castle, Castleton, Near Lostwithiel, PL22 0BD
t: (01208) 872687   **w:** english-heritage.org.uk/restormel

open: See website for details.
admission: £2.40

description: Surrounded by a deep, dry moat and perched on a high mound, the huge circular keep of this Norman castle survives in good condition.

facilities:

Prideaux Place

Prideaux Place, Padstow, PL28 8RP
t: (01841) 532411   **w:** prideauxplace.co.uk

open:	May–Oct, Mon–Thu, Sun 1230–1700.
admission:	£7.00

description: A 16thC Elizabethan mansion with contemporary embossed plaster ceiling in the Great Chamber. Forty acres of grounds including deer park.

facilities: 💭 🍴 ♿

Cotehele

Cotehele, St Dominick, PL12 6TA
t: (01579) 351346   **w:** nationaltrust.org.uk

open:	Mar–Oct, Mon–Thu, Sat–Sun 1100–1630.
admission:	£8.00

description: Medieval house with superb collections of textiles, armour and furniture, set in extensive grounds. Home of the Edgcumbe family for centuries, its granite and slatestone walls contain intimate chambers adorned with tapestries.

facilities: 💭 🐕 ⛩ ♿

Saint Mawes Castle

St Mawes Castle, St Mawes, TR2 3AA
t: (01326) 270526   **w:** english-heritage.org.uk/stmawes

open:	See website for details.
admission:	£3.60
description:	On edge of Roseland Peninsula, erected by Henry VIII for coastal defence. Clover-leaf shaped and still intact. Fine example of military architecture. Lovely gardens.
facilities:	⚔ ⛱ ♿

King Arthur Great Halls

King Arthur's Great Halls, Fore Street, Tintagel, PL34 0DA
t: (01840) 770526   **w:** kingarthursgreathalls.com

open:	Summer: daily 1000–1700. Winter: daily 1100–1500.
admission:	£3.50
description:	Dedicated to the Arthurian legend, this is the home of Robert Powell's narrated light show about the deeds of the Knights of the Round Table.

facilities:	🐕 ♿

TINTAGEL

Tintagel Castle

Tintagel Castle, Tintagel, PL34 0HE
t: (01840) 770328 **w:** english-heritage.org.uk/tintagel

open: See website for details.
admission: £4.30

description: Medieval ruined castle on wild, wind-swept coast. Famous for associations with Arthurian legend. Built largely in 13thC by Richard, Earl of Cornwall.

facilities:

WASHAWAY

Pencarrow House and Gardens

Pencarrow House and Gardens, Washaway, PL30 3AG
t: (01208) 841369 **w:** pencarrow.co.uk

open: Apr–Oct, Mon–Thu, Sun 1100–1700.
admission: £8.00

description: Historic Georgian house, superb collection of paintings, furniture and china. Extensive grounds, picnic area, craft centre, children's play area and pets' corner, tearooms.

facilities:

Hill Top

Hill Top, Nr Sawrey, Ambleside, LA22 0LF
t: (015394) 36269   **w:** nationaltrust.org.uk

open:	Apr–May, Mon–Wed, Sat–Sun 1030–1630. Jun–Aug, Mon–Thu, Sat–Sun 1030–1630. Sep–Oct, Mon–Wed, Sat–Sun 1030–1630.
admission:	£5.10
description:	Delightful, small 17thC house where Beatrix Potter wrote many of her famous children's stories. View her personal treasures.
facilities:	🐕

Rydal Mount and Gardens

Rydal Mount and Gardens, Rydal, Ambleside, LA22 9LU
t: (015394) 33002   **w:** rydalmount.co.uk

open:	Apr–Oct, daily 0930–1700. Nov–Dec, Mon, Wed–Sun 0930–1700.
admission:	£5.00
description:	Wordsworth's best-loved home for 37 years. It was here that he wrote many of his poems. He became Poet Laureate to Queen Victoria at the age of 74.
facilities:	🐕

Carlisle Castle

Carlisle Castle, Carlisle, CA3 8UR
t: (01228) 591922   **w:** english-heritage.org.uk

open:	See website for details.
admission:	£4.10

description: This 12thC castle has a bloody and fascinating past. Mary Queen of Scots was imprisoned here. From the castle

there is a commanding view of historic Carlisle.

facilities: 🐕 ♿

Brantwood, Home of John Ruskin

Brantwood, Home of John Ruskin, Coniston, LA21 8AD
t: (015394) 41396   **w:** brantwood.org.uk

open: Apr–Oct, daily 1100–1730. Nov–Mar, Wed–Sun 1100–1630.
admission: £5.95

description: Brantwood, the former home of John Ruskin, is most beautifully situated, with fine lake and mountain views from its 250-acre estate.

facilities: 🐕 ♿

Holker Hall and Gardens GRANGE-OVER-SANDS

Holker Hall and Gardens, Cark-in-Cartmel,
Grange-over-Sands, LA11 7PL
t: (015395) 58328   **w:** holker-hall.co.uk

open:	Gardens: Apr–Oct, Mon–Fri, Sun 1030–1730.
	Hall: Apr–Oct, Mon–Fri, Sun 1200–1600.
admission:	£9.25
description:	Magnificent hall, award-winning gardens and museum - three attractions in one setting. There is also the Courtyard cafe, food hall and free parking.
facilities:	�Ⓟ 🏃 🛋 ♿

Dove Cottage and The Wordsworth Museum GRASMERE

Dove Cottage and The Wordsworth Museum,
Dove Cottage, Grasmere, LA22 9SH   **t:** (015394) 35544
w: wordsworth.org.uk

open:	All year, daily 0930–1730.
admission:	£6.20
description:	Wordsworth's home during his most creative period. Guided cottage tours, award-winning museum displaying manuscripts, portraits, paintings and memorabilia.
facilities:	▐ 🏃 🛋 ♿

Levens Hall & Gardens

Levens Hall & Gardens, Levens, Kendal, LA8 0PD
t: (015395) 60321   **w:** levenshall.co.uk

open: Gardens: Apr–Sep, Mon–Thu, Sun 1000–1700.
House: Apr–Sep, Mon–Thu, Sun 1200–1600.
admission: £9.50

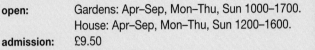

description: Elizabethan mansion and world-famous topiary gardens designed by M Beaumont in 1694. Fountain garden and nuttery, licensed restaurant and gift shop.

facilities: ☕ 🏃 ♿

Sizergh Castle and Garden

Sizergh Castle and Garden, Sizergh, Kendal, LA8 8AE
t: (015395) 60951   **w:** nationaltrust.org.uk

open: Castle: Apr–Oct, Mon–Thu, Sun 1300–1700.
Garden: Apr–Oct, Mon–Thu, Sun 1100–1700.
admission: £6.20

description: Occupied by the Strickland family for over 760 years. View some of the finest Elizabethan carved overmantels, English and French furniture and Jacobite relics.

facilities: ☕ 🏃 🪑

Mirehouse Historic House and Gardens

Mirehouse Historic House and Gardens, Underskiddaw, Keswick, CA12 4QE   **t:** (01768) 772287   **w:** mirehouse.com

open:	House: Apr–Oct, Sun, Wed 1400–1700.
	Gardens: Apr–Oct, daily 1000–1700.
admission:	£2.60
description:	Family-run historic house with strong literary connections in a spectacular location. Four playgrounds, beautiful gardens and tearoom.
facilities:	☕ ✗

Dalemain Historic House & Gardens

Dalemain Historic House & Gardens, Dalemain, Penrith, CA11 0HB   **t:** (01768) 486450   **w:** dalemain.com

open:	Gardens: Apr–Oct, Mon–Thu, Sun 1030–1700. Nov–Mar, Mon–Thu, Sun 1100–1600. House: Apr–Oct, Mon–Thu, Sun 1115–1600.
admission:	£6.50
description:	A medieval, Tudor and early-Georgian house. Guided tours available. Wonderful five-acre plantsman garden set against the splendour of the Lakeland Fells.
facilities:	☕ ✗

Muncaster

Muncaster, Muncaster Castle, Ravenglass, CA18 1RQ
t: (01229) 717614   **w:** muncaster.co.uk

open:	Gardens, Owl Centre, Meadowvole Maze: 11 Feb–4 Nov 1030–1800. Castle: 11 Feb–4 Nov, Sun–Fri 1200–1700.
admission:	£9.50
description:	Historic haunted castle with extensive gardens and glorious views. Headquarters of the World Owl Trust with daily bird show. Meadowvole Maze. Gift shops, cafe, plant centre. Magical winter evenings with darkest Muncaster!
facilities:	

Blackwell, The Arts & Craft House

Blackwell, The Arts & Craft House, Bowness-on-Windermere, Windermere, LA23 3JT   **t:** (015394) 46139
w: blackwell.org.uk

open:	Apr–Oct, daily 1030–1700. Nov–Dec, daily 1030–1600.
admission:	£5.45
description:	Elegant arts and crafts house and gardens with spectacular views across Windermere. The restored interiors include many original features. Changing exhibitions of craft in upper galleries.
facilities:	

Chatsworth House, Garden, Farmyard & Adventure Playground

Chatsworth House, Garden, Farmyard & Adventure
Playground, Chatsworth, Bakewell, DE45 1PP
t: (01246) 582204 **w:** chatsworth.org

open: House: Mar–Dec, daily
1100–1730. Garden: Mar–Dec, daily
1100–1800. Farmyard: Mar–Dec,
daily 1030–1730.
admission: £11.00

description: Visitors to Chatsworth see more than 30 richly
decorated rooms, the garden with fountains,
a cascade and maze and the farmyard and
adventure playground.

facilities: ☕ ✕ ♿

Haddon Hall

Haddon Hall, Haddon Estate Office, Bakewell,
DE45 1LA **t:** (01629) 812855 **w:** haddonhall.co.uk

open: Apr, Mon, Sat–Sun 1200–1700. May–Sep,
daily 1200–1700. Oct, Mon, Sat–Sun 1200–
1700.
admission: £8.50

description: Magnificent medieval
and Tudor manor house,
virtually untouched
since the reign of
Henry VIII. Outstanding
terraced gardens.
Popular film and
television location.

facilities: ✕ ♿

Bolsover Castle

BOLSOVER

Bolsover Castle, Castle Street, Bolsover, S44 6PR
t: (01246) 822844   **w:** english-heritage.org.uk

open:	Apr, Mon, Thu–Fri 1000–1700, Sat 1000–1600. May–Sep, Mon–Fri, Sun 1000–1800, Sat 1000–1600. Oct, Mon, Thu–Fri, Sun 1000–1700, Sat 1000–1600. Nov–Mar, Mon, Thu–Sun 1000–1600.
admission:	£6.80

description: A 17thC house built on the site of a Norman fortress - enchanting, romantic and magical.

facilities: 🖥 🏹 🪑 ♿

Peveril Castle

CASTLETON

Peveril Castle, Market Place, Castleton, S33 8WQ
t: (01433) 620613   **w:** english-heritage.org.uk

open:	Apr, daily 1000–1700. May–Aug, daily 1000–1800. Sep–Oct, daily 1000–1700. Nov–Mar, Mon, Thu–Sun 1000–1600.
admission:	£3.50

description: A ruined Norman castle on the hill high above Castleton, built in the 11thC. The curtain wall is almost complete with a small imposing keep.

facilities: 🐕 ♿

Hardwick Hall

DOE LEA

Hardwick Hall, Doe Lea, S44 5QJ
t: (01246) 850430   **w:** nationaltrust.org.uk

open:	Apr–Oct, Wed–Thu, Sat–Sun 1200–1630.
admission:	£9.00

description: Elizabethan country house, gardens and parkland, with outstanding collections of furniture, tapestry and needlework.

facilities: ◨ ⚔ ⛺ ♿

Kedleston Hall

KEDLESTON

Kedleston Hall, Kedleston, DE22 5JH
t: (01332) 842191   **w:** nationaltrust.org.uk

open:	Hall: Apr–Oct, Mon–Wed, Sat–Sun 1200–1630. Park: Apr–Oct, daily 1000–1800. Nov–Feb, daily 1000–1600.
admission:	£8.00

description: An outstanding Robert Adam house, 1759-1765, with a unique marble hall, saloon, state rooms, Old Masters, furniture, Lord Curzon's Indian museum, a 12thC church and a park.

facilities: ◨ ⚔ ⛺

Melbourne Hall: Gardens and Visitor Centre

MELBOURNE

Melbourne Hall: Gardens and Visitor Centre, Melbourne, DE73 1EN   **t:** (01332) 862502   **w:** melbournehall.com

open:	Hall: Aug, daily 1400–1630. Gardens: Apr–Sep, Wed, Sat–Sun, Bank Hols 1330–1730.
admission:	£3.50
description:	Queen Victoria's Prime Minister, Lord Melbourne, lived here as did Byron's friend Lady Caroline Lamb. There are famous formal gardens and a visitor centre.
facilities:	▆ 🏃 ♿

Sudbury Hall (National Trust)

SUDBURY

Sudbury Hall (National Trust), Sudbury, DE6 5HT
t: (01283) 585305   **w:** nationaltrust.org.uk

open:	Apr–Oct, Wed–Sun 1300–1700.
admission:	£6.30
description:	A grand 17thC house with plasterwork ceilings, ceiling paintings, a carved staircase and overmantel. The Museum of Childhood is in the old servants' wing.
facilities:	▆ 🏃 ⛱

Calke Abbey, Park and Gardens

Calke Abbey, Park and Gardens, Ticknall, DE73 1LE
t: (01332) 863822   **w:** nationaltrust.org.uk

open:	House: Mar–Oct, Mon–Wed, Sat–Sun 1230–1700. Garden: Apr–Oct, Mon–Wed, Sat–Sun 1100–1700. Jul–Aug, daily 1100–1700.
admission:	£8.00

description: Built 1701-1703, and largely unchanged in 100 years. Natural-history collections, 750 acres of park, ponds, trees, woodlands, walled gardens and pleasure gardens.

facilities:

Arlington Court

Arlington Court, Arlington, EX31 4LP
t: (01271) 850296   **w:** nationaltrust.org.uk

open:	Mar–Oct, Mon–Fri, Sun 1030–1700.
admission:	£7.00

description: Historic house with interesting collection. Gardens with rhododendrons, azaleas and hydrangeas. Carriage collection and rides. Extensive estate walks.

facilities:

Berry Pomeroy Castle

Berry Pomeroy Castle, Berry Pomeroy, TQ9 6NJ
t: (01803) 866618   **w:** english-heritage.org.uk/berrypomeroy

open:	Apr–Jun, Oct, daily 1000–1700. Jul–Aug, daily 1000–1800. Sep, daily 1000–1700.
admission:	£3.60
description:	A romantic ruined castle set in a picturesque Devon valley. The gatehouse dates from the late 15thC with Elizabethan remains behind. Steeped in folklore.
facilities:	☕ 🏃 ♿

Killerton House and Garden

Killerton House and Garden, Broadclyst, EX5 3LE
t: (01392) 881345   **w:** nationaltrust.org.uk

open:	See website for details.
admission:	£5.80
description:	An 18thC house built for the Acland family. Hillside garden of 18 acres with rare trees and shrubs.
facilities:	☕ 🏃 🪑 ♿

Ugbrooke House and Park

Ugbrooke House and Park, Chudleigh, TQ13 0AD
t: (01626) 852179   **w:** ugbrooke.co.uk

open: Jul–Sep, Tue, Wed, Thur, Sun, Bank Hols
1300–1730.

admission: £6.00

description: Robert Adam-designed house and chapel, Capability Brown-designed park and grounds. Fine furniture, paintings, needlework, costume and uniforms.

facilities:

Dartmouth Castle

Dartmouth Castle, Castle Road, Dartmouth, TQ6 0JN
t: (01803) 833588
w: english-heritage.org.uk/dartmouth

open: Apr–Jun, Sep, daily
1000–1700, Jul–Aug, daily
1000–1800, Oct–Mar daily
1000–1600.

admission: £3.70

description: This brilliantly positioned defensive castle juts out into the narrow entrance to the Dart Estuary. One of the first castles constructed with artillery in mind.

facilities:

Castle Drogo

Castle Drogo, Drewsteignton, EX6 6PB
t: (01647) 433306   **w:** nationaltrust.org.uk

open:	Mar–Oct, Wed–Sun 1100–1700. Dec, Sat–Sun 1200–1600.
admission:	£7.40

 **description:** Granite castle, built between 1910 and 1930 by Sir Edwin Lutyens, standing at over 900ft overlooking the wooded gorge of the River Teign. Views of Dartmoor.

facilities:

Hartland Abbey and Gardens

Hartland Abbey and Gardens, Hartland, EX39 6DT
t: (01237) 441234   **w:** hartlandabbey.com

open:	Apr–May, Wed–Thur, Sun and Bank Hols 1230–1700. May–Sep, Mon–Thur, Sun 1230–1700.
admission:	£8.00
description:	Family home since the dissolution in 1539. Woodland gardens leading to bog garden and 18th century walled gardens. Beautiful walk to beach.

facilities:

Hemyock Castle

Hemyock Castle, Hemyock, EX15 3RJ
t: (01823) 680745   **w:** hemyockcastle.co.uk

open: Mar–Sep, Bank Hols 1400–1700.

description: Medieval moated castle and gatehouse remains. Interpretation centre illustrating the history of the site. Life-size historical tableaux including extended Civil War display.

facilities:

Tapeley Park

Tapeley Park, Instow, EX39 4NT
t: (01271) 342558   **w:** tapeleypark.com

open: Mar–Oct 1000–1700.
admission: £4.00

description: Devon home of the Christie family of Glyndebourne, overlooking the estuary to the sea. Beautiful Italian garden with many rare plants and woodland walk.

facilities:

Powderham Castle

Powderham Castle, Kenton, EX6 8JQ
t: (01626) 890243   **w:** powderham.co.uk

open: Apr–Oct, daily 1000–1730.
admission: £7.95

description: Built c1390 and restored in the 18thC. Georgian interiors, china, furnishings and paintings. Family home of the Courtenays for over 600 years. Fine views across deer park and River Exe.

facilities:

Okehampton Castle

Okehampton Castle, Castle Lodge, Okehampton, EX20 1JB
t: (01837) 52844   **w:** english-heritage.org.uk/okehampton

open: Apr–Jun, daily 1000–1700, Jul–Aug, daily 1000–1800, Sep, daily 1000–1700.
admission: £3.00

description: The ruins of the largest castle in Devon, including the jagged remains of the keep. Picnic area and enchanted woodland walks.

facilities:

Cadhay

Cadhay, Ottery St Mary, EX11 1QT
t: (01404) 812432   **w:** cadhay.org.uk

open:	May–Sep, Fri 1400–1730.
admission:	£2.00

description: Historic Elizabethan manorhouse built c1550 around a courtyard. Fine timber roof of Great Hall and Elizabethan Long Gallery. Magnificent gardens.

facilities: ☕ 🍴 ♿

Saltram

Saltram, Plympton, PL7 1UH
t: (01752) 333500   **w:** nationaltrust.org.uk

open:	See website for details.
admission:	£8.00

description: George II mansion with magnificent interiors designed by Robert Adam. Fine period furniture, china and paintings. Garden with orangery. Art gallery and play area.

facilities: ☕ 🍴 ⛱ ♿

Knightshayes Court

Knightshayes Court, Bolham, Tiverton, EX16 7RQ
t: (01884) 254665   **w:** nationaltrust.org.uk

open:	Mar–Nov, Mon–Thu, Sat–Sun 1100–1700.
admission:	£5.50

description:	House built c1870 by William Burges. Celebrated garden features a water lily pool, topiary, fine specimen trees, formal terraces, spring bulbs and rare shrubs.

facilities:

Tiverton Castle

Tiverton Castle, Park Hill, Tiverton, EX16 6RP
t: (01884) 253200   **w:** tivertoncastle.com

open:	Apr–Oct, Thu, Sun, Bank Hols 1430–1730.
admission:	£4.00

description:	All ages of architecture from medieval to modern. Important Civil War armoury - try some on. Beautiful gardens with romantic ruins.

facilities:

Totnes Castle

Totnes Castle, Castle Street, Totnes, TQ9 5NU
t: (01803) 864406   **w:** english-heritage.org.uk/totnes

open:	Apr–Jun, daily 1000–1700. Jul–Aug, daily 1000–1600. Sep, daily 1000–1700. Oct, daily 1000–1600.
admission:	£2.40

description: One of the best-preserved Norman shell keeps, this motte and bailey castle offers splendid views over the River Dart.

facilities: ✕

Buckland Abbey

Buckland Abbey, Yelverton, PL20 6EY
t: (01822) 853607   **w:** nationaltrust.org.uk

open:	See website for details.
admission:	£7.00

description: Originally a Cistercian monastery, then home of Sir Francis Drake. Ancient buildings, exhibitions, herb garden, craft workshops and estate walks. Elizabethan garden.

facilities: ▣ ✕ ⊼ ♿

Athelhampton House and Gardens

Athelhampton House and Gardens,
Athelhampton, DT2 7LG
t: (01305) 848363   **w:** athelhampton.co.uk

open:	Apr–Oct, Mar, Mon–Thu, Sun 1030–1700. Nov–Feb, Sun 1030–1700.
admission:	£8.50
description:	Legendary site of King Athelstan's palace. One of the finest 15thC manorhouses, surrounded by glorious Grade I Listed garden with fountains, pools and waterfalls.
facilities:	▆ ⚔ 🗑 ♿

Christchurch Castle

Christchurch Castle, Castle Street, Christchurch
t: (01202) 495127   **w:** visitchristchurch.info

open:	Daily.
description:	Late 11th century castle built to protect the town.
facilities:	🐕

Corfe Castle

Corfe Castle, The Square, Corfe Castle, BH20 5EZ
t: (01929) 477063   w: nationaltrust.org.uk

open:	Apr–Sep, daily 1000–1800. Nov–Feb, daily 1000–1600. March, Oct, daily 1000–1700.
admission:	£5.00
description:	Ruins of former royal castle sieged and slighted in 1646 by parliamentary forces.
facilities:	☕ 🐕 ♿

Edmondsham House and Garden

Edmondsham House and Garden, Edmondsham House, Edmondsham, Cranborne, BH21 5RE
t: (01725) 517207

open:	House: Apr, Wed 1400–1700. Oct, Wed 1400–1700. Bank Hols, 1400–1700. Gardens: Apr–Oct, Wed, Sun 1400–1700.
admission:	£4.00
description:	Fine Tudor/Georgian manorhouse, with Victorian stables and dairy. Six-acre garden and one-acre walled garden.
facilities:	☕ 🏹 ⛩ ♿

Max Gate

Max Gate, Alington Avenue, Dorchester, DT1 2AA
t: (01305) 262538   **w:** maxgate.co.uk

open:	Apr–Sep, Mon, Weds, Sun 1400–1700.
admission:	£3.00

description:	Victorian house designed by Thomas Hardy, and his home from 1885 until his death in 1928. Contains several pieces of Hardy's furniture.

facilities: 🐕 ♿

Highcliffe Castle

Highcliffe Castle, Rothesay Drive, off Lymington Road,
Highcliffe, BH23 4LE   **t:** (01425) 278807
w: highcliffecastle.co.uk

open:	Feb–Dec, daily 1100–1700.
admission:	£2.20

description: Grade I Listed c1830 picturesque and romantic seaside mansion. Now fully repaired to exterior only. Six staterooms open as visitor and exhibition centre.

facilities: ☕ 🏃 ⛱ ♿

Hardy's Cottage

HIGHER BOCKHAMPTON

Hardy's Cottage, Higher Bockhampton, DT2 8QJ
t: (01297) 561900   **w:** nationaltrust.org.uk

open:	Apr–Oct, Mon–Thu, Sun 1100–1700.
admission:	£3.50

description: Thomas Hardy was born here in 1840. It is where he wrote 'Under the Greenwood Tree' and 'Far from the Madding Crowd'.

facilities:

Bishop's and Earl's Palaces

KIRKWALL

Bishop's and Earl's Palaces, Watergate, Kirkwall, KW15 1PD
t: (01856) 871918   **w:** historic-scotland.gov.uk

open:	Apr–Sep, Mon–Sun 0930–1730. Oct, Sat–Wed 0930–1630.
admission:	£3.50

description: The Bishop's Palace dates from the 12th century, with a round tower built by Bishop Reid in the 16th century. The adjacent Earl's Palace was built in the 17th century by Patrick Stewart.

facilities:

Portland Castle

Portland Castle, Portland, DT5 1AZ
t: (01305) 820539   w: english-heritage.org.uk/portlandcastle

open:	Apr–June, daily 1000–1700. Jul–Aug, daily 1000–1800. Sep, daily 1000–1700. Oct, daily 1000–1600.
admission:	£3.80
description:	A well-preserved coastal fort built by Henry VIII to defend Weymouth Harbour against possible French and Spanish attack. Exhibition detailing 400 years of the castle's history.
facilities:	☕ 🏃 ♿

Sherborne Castle

Sherborne Castle, Sherborne Castle Estates, New Road,
Sherborne, DT9 5NR   t: (01935) 813182
w: sherbornecastle.com

open:	Apr–Oct, Tue–Thur, Sat–Sun, Bank Hols 1100–1630.
admission:	£4.00
description:	Built by Sir Walter Raleigh in 1594. Home to the Digby family since 1617. Splendid collections of decorative arts. Capability Brown lake, gardens and grounds.
facilities:	☕ 🐕 ⛱ ♿

Lulworth Castle & Park

Lulworth Castle & Park, East Lulworth, Wareham, BH20 5QS
t: 0845 450 1054   **w:** lulworth.com

open:	Summer: Sun–Fri 1030–1800. Winter: Sun–Fri 1030–1600 (excl 24–25 Dec, 7–20 Jan).
admission:	£7.00
description:	Idyllic castle set in extensive park with 18thC chapel, animal farm, adventure play area, woodland walks, picnic area, cafe and courtyard shop. Special events throughout the year including The Knights of Lulworth.
facilities:	▱ 🐕 🇦 ♿

Kingston Lacy House and Gardens

Kingston Lacy House and Gardens, Wimborne Minster, BH21 4EA   **t:** (01202) 883402   **w:** nationaltrust.org.uk

open:	House: Apr–Oct, Wed–Sun 1100–1600. Gardens: Apr–Oct, daily 1030–1800. Nov–Dec, Fri–Sun 1030–1600. Feb–Mar, Sat–Sun 1030–1600.

admission:	£9.00
description:	A 17thC house designed for Sir Ralph Bankes by Sir Roger Pratt, altered by Sir Charles Barry in the 19thC. Collection of paintings, 250-acre wooded park, herd of Devon cattle.
facilities:	▱ ⚒ 🇦 ♿

Barnard Castle

Barnard Castle, Barnard Castle, DL12 8PR
t: (01833) 638212   **w:** english-heritage.org.uk

open:	Apr–Sep, daily 1000–1800. Oct, daily 1000–1600. Nov–Mar, Mon, Thu–Sun 1000–1600.
admission:	£3.40

description: A ruined castle overlooking the River Tees. Remains include the 14thC great hall, the three-storey keep and the circular round tower which inspired Sir Walter Scott (Rokeby).

facilities: 🐕 ⛱ ♿

Bowes Castle

Bowes Castle, Bowes, Barnard Castle, DL12 9HP
t: (01833) 638212   **w:** english-heritage.org.uk

open:	Daily.
description:	Three-storey-high stone keep, dating from 1170 and set within the earthworks of a Roman fort, guarding the strategic Stainmore pass over the Pennines.
facilities:	🐕

Rokeby Park

Rokeby Park, Rokeby, Barnard Castle, DL12 9RZ
t: (01833) 690100   **w:** rokebypark.com

open:	May–Sep, Mon–Tue 1400–1700.
admission:	£5.00

description: A beautiful Palladian-style country house which was the setting for Sir Walter Scott's ballad 'Rokeby', containing a unique collection of 18thC needlework and period furniture.

facilities: ✗ ♿

Auckland Castle

Auckland Castle, Bishop Auckland, DL14 7NR
t: (01388) 601627   **w:** auckland-castle.co.uk

open:	Apr–Jun, Mon, Sun 1400–1700. Jul–Aug, Mon, Wed 1100–1700, Sun 1400–1700. Sept, Mon, Sun 1400–1700.
admission:	£4.00

description: Principal country residence of the Prince Bishops since 1190, the castle is now home to the Bishop of Durham. Visit St Peter's Chapel, state rooms and deer park.

facilities: ✗ ♿

Raby Castle

Raby Castle, Staindrop, Darlington, DL2 3AH
t: (01833) 660202   **w:** rabycastle.com

open:	Castle: May–Jun, Sep, Wed, Sun 1300–1700. Jul–Aug, Mon–Fri, Sun 1300–1700. Bank Hols including Sat 1300–1700. Park & Gardens: May–Jun, Sept, Wed, Sun 1100–1730. Jul–Aug, Mon–Fri, Sun 1100–1730. Bank Hols including Sat 1100–1730.
admission:	£9.00
description:	The medieval castle, home of Lord Barnard's family since 1626, includes a 200-acre deer park, walled gardens, carriage collection, adventure playground, shop and tearoom.
facilities:	▬ ⋔ ⊼ ⧠

Croxdale Hall

Croxdale Hall, Durham, DH6 5JP
t: (0191) 378 0911

open:	Please phone for details.
description:	Croxdale, home to the Salvin family since 1402, stands boldly over the River Wear. Mid-Georgian rooms with fine rococo ceilings, chapel, walled gardens and orangery.
facilities:	⋔ ⧠

Durham Castle

Durham Castle, Palace Green, Durham, DH1 3RW   t: (0191) 334 4106
w: durhamcastle.com

open: Apr–Sep, daily 1000–1200, 1400–1630. Oct–Mar, Mon, Wed, Sat–Sun 1400–1600.
admission: £5.00

description: Castle founded in 1072. Norman chapel dating from 1080. Kitchens and great hall dating from 1499 and 1284 respectively. A fine example of a motte-and-bailey castle.

facilities: ✗

Maister House

Maister House, 160 High Street, Hull, HU1 1NL
t: (01482) 324114   w: nationaltrust.org.uk

open: All year, Mon–Fri 1000–1600.

description: This Georgian merchant's house was rebuilt in 1743 in the Palladian manner, acting as an impressive symbol of Hull's 18thC heyday. Superb staircase and hall with ironwork by Bakewell.

facilities: ✗

Wilberforce House

Wilberforce House, 25 High Street, Hull, HU1 1NQ
t: (01482) 613902   **w:** hullcc.gov.uk/museums

open: All year, Mon–Sat 1000–1700, Sun 1330–1630.

description: The birthplace of William Wilberforce, Hull MP and slavery abolitionist whose campaign made the establishment of Freetown (Sierra Leone) possible. Slavery exhibits, period rooms and furniture.

facilities:

Wassand Hall, Gardens & Grounds

Wassand Hall, Gardens & Grounds, Seaton, HU11 5RJ
t: (01964) 534488   **w:** wassand.co.uk

open: See website for details.
admission: £5.00

description: A fine Regency house in beautiful tranquil surroundings, containing 18thC and 19thC paintings and a collection of English and European silver, furniture and porcelain from the same period.

facilities:

Sewerby Hall and Gardens

SEWERBY

Sewerby Hall and Gardens, Church Lane, Sewerby, YO15 1EA   **t:** (01262) 673769   **w:** bridlington.net/sewerby

open:	Hall: Apr–Oct, daily 1000–1700. Gardens: Daily, dawn–dusk.
admission:	£3.80
description:	Situated in a dramatic cliff-top position, forming the gateway to the Flamborough Heritage Coast, Sewerby Hall and Gardens, set in 50 acres of early 19thC parkland, enjoys spectacular views over Bridlington.
facilities:	☕ 🐕 🪑 ♿

Sledmere House

SLEDMERE

Sledmere House, Sledmere, YO25 3XG
t: (01377) 236637

open:	May, Tue–Thu, Sun 1100–1700. Jun–Aug, Tue–Fri, Sun, Bank Hols 1100–1700. Sep, Tue–Thu, Sun 1100–1700.
admission:	£6.00
description:	Georgian house containing Chippendale, Sheraton and French furnishing and many fine pictures. Magnificent plasterwork by Joseph Rose (Adam style). Capability Brown parkland, woodland walks, rose and knot gardens, chapel.

facilities:	☕ 🐕 🪑 ♿

Alfriston Clergy House

Alfriston Clergy House, The Tye, Alfriston, BN26 5TL
t: (01323) 870001   **w:** nationaltrust.org.uk

open:	Apr–Oct, Mon, Wed–Thu, Sat–Sun 1000–1700. Nov–Dec, Mon, Wed–Thu, Sat–Sun 1100–1600.
admission:	£3.60
description:	A beautiful thatched medieval hall house, the first building to be acquired by the National Trust in 1896. Pretty cottage garden with a charming gift shop.
facilities:	⚞ ⏃ ♿

Preston Manor

Preston Manor, Preston Park, Brighton, BN1 6SD
t: (01273) 292770   **w:** virtualmuseum.info

open:	Apr–Sep, Tue–Sat 1000–1700, Sun 1400–1700.
admission:	£4.00

description:	A delightful manor house with the interior of an Edwardian home containing ceramics, furniture, glass, clocks and silver. Servants' quarters and restored kitchen. Garden.
facilities:	⚞ ⏃ ♿

Royal Pavilion

BRIGHTON

Royal Pavilion, Brighton, BN1 1EE
t: (01273) 290900   **w:** royalpavilion.org.uk

open:	Apr–Sep, daily 0930–1745. Oct–Mar, daily 1000–1715.
admission:	£7.50

description: The Royal Pavilion is the magnificent former seaside residence of King George IV. It is decorated in Chinese taste and has an Indian exterior.

facilities: ◼ 🍴 ⚒ ♿

Bateman's

BURWASH

Bateman's, Burwash, TN19 7DS
t: (01435) 882302   **w:** nationaltrust.org.uk

open:	House: Apr–Oct, Mon–Wed, Sat–Sun 1100–1700. Gardens: Apr–Oct, Mon–Wed, Sat–Sun 1100–1730. Nov–Dec, Wed–Sun 1100–1600.
admission:	£6.85

description: A 17thC ironmaster's house which was the home of Rudyard Kipling between 1902 and 1935. His study and Rolls Royce can be seen. Garden with working watermill.

facilities: ◼ 🍴 ♿

Charleston

Charleston, The Charleston Trust, Charleston, Firle, BN8 6LL
t: (01323) 811265   **w:** charleston.org.uk

open:	Mar–Jun, Sep–Oct, Wed, Sat 1130–1700, Thu, Fri, Sun, Bank Hols 1400–1700. Jul–Aug, Wed–Sat 1130–1700, Sun, Bank Hols 1400–1700.
admission:	£6.50
description:	A 17th-18thC farmhouse, home of Vanessa Bell and Duncan Grant of the Bloomsbury set. House and contents decorated by the artists. Traditional walled garden.
facilities:	☕ ✗ ♿

Firle Place

Firle Place, Firle, BN8 6LP
t: (01273) 858307   **w:** firleplace.co.uk

open:	Jun–Sep, Wed–Thu, Sun, Bank Hols 1400–1615.
admission:	£6.00
description:	A Tudor house with Georgian additions in a downland park setting. Important English and European Old Master paintings, fine furniture and notable Sevres porcelain.
facilities:	☕ ✗ ♿

Glynde Place

Glynde Place, Glynde, BN8 6SX
t: (01273) 858224   **w:** glyndeplace.com

open:	May–Aug, Wed, Sun, Bank Hols 1400–1700.
admission:	£6.00
description:	A 16thC Sussex brick and flint house around a courtyard. Interior features include a panelled Long Gallery, old masters' portraits, furniture, embroidery and 18thC bronzes.
facilities:	☕ ✗ ♿

Hammerwood Park

Hammerwood Park, Hammerwood, RH19 3QE
t: (01342) 850594   **w:** mistral.co.uk/hammerwood

open:	Jun–Sep, Wed, Sat, Bank Hols 1400–1730.
admission:	£6.00
description:	House built in 1792 by Latrobe, White House architect, and now being restored. The interior contains varied furniture, a copy of the Elgin marbles and musical instruments.
facilities:	☕ ✗ ♿

Bolebroke Castle

Bolebroke Castle, Edenbridge Road, Hartfield, TN7 4JJ
t: (01892) 770061   **w:** bolebrokecastle.co.uk

open:	All year, daily 1100–1600.
admission:	£5.00

description: Tudor castle in beautiful 30-acre estate. Used by Henry VIII as a hunting lodge, and scene of his courting of Anne Boleyn. Contains the second largest fireplace in England and a magnificent Elizabethan staircase.

facilities: ▣ ✕ 𐀀 ♿

Hastings Castle and 1066 Story

Hastings Castle and 1066 Story, West Hill, Hastings, TN34 3HY   **t:** (01424) 781112   **w:** discoverhastings.co.uk

open:	Apr–Jul, daily 0900–1700. Aug–Sep, daily 1000–1730. Oct–Mar, daily 1000–1600.
admission:	£3.75

description: Fragmentary remains of Norman Castle built on West Hill after William the Conqueror's victory at the Battle of Hastings. 1066 Story interpretation centre in siege tent.

facilities: ✕ 𐀀 ♿

Lewes Castle and Barbican House Museum

Lewes Castle and Barbican House Museum,
Barbican House, 169 High Street, Lewes, BN7 1YE
t: (01273) 486290   **w:** sussexpast.co.uk

open: All year, Mon 1100–1730,
Tue–Sat 1000–1730, Sun,
Bank Hols 1100–1730.

admission: £4.70

description: Historic display interpreting
Lewes with indoor audiovisual programme
and scale-model of the town c120 years ago.
Norman castle remains. History of Lewes from
Saxon times.

facilities: ✗

Great Dixter House and Gardens

Great Dixter House and Gardens, Northiam, TN31 6PH
t: (01797) 252878   **w:** greatdixter.co.uk

open: House: Apr–Oct, Tue–Sun, Bank
Hols 1400–1700. Gardens: Apr–Oct,
Tue–Sun, Bank Hols 1100–1700.
admission: £7.50

description: An example of a 15thC manor house with
antique furniture and needlework. Home of
gardening writer Christopher Lloyd. The house
is restored and the gardens were designed by
Lutyens.

facilities: ✗ ⛱ ♿

Pevensey Castle

Pevensey Castle, High Street, Pevensey, BN24 5LE
t: (01323) 762604   **w:** english-heritage.org.uk

open:	Apr–Sep, daily 1000–1800. Oct, Sat–Sun 1000–1600.
admission:	£3.90

description:	A Roman fortress built in 4thC as a defence against Saxon pirates, includes fine west gate. Norman castle built within Roman walls contains remains of unusual keep. Tudor gun.

facilities:

Old Mint House

The Old Mint House, High Street, Pevensey, BN24 5LF
t: (01323) 762337   **w:** minthouse.co.uk

open:	All year, Mon–Fri 0900–1700.
admission:	£1.50

description:	A house built c1342 on the site of an old mint, featuring 14thC carvings and frescos. A bedroom used by King Edward VI can be seen.

facilities:

Monks House

RODMELL

Monks House, Rodmell, BN7 3HF
t: (01372) 453401   **w:** nationaltrust.org.uk

open: Apr–Oct, Wed, Sat 1400–1730.
admission: £3.30

description: Small converted farmhouse, home to Virginia
                 Woolf and her husband Leonard from 1919
                 until his death in 1969. Furniture and personal
                 items, garden and summerhouse.

facilities: 🐕 ⛩ ♿

Lamb House

RYE

Lamb House, West Street, Rye, TN31 7ES
t: (01797) 229542   **w:** nationaltrust.org.uk

open: Apr–Oct, Thu, Sat 1400–1800.
admission: £3.30

description: Early Georgian house and
walled garden, home of writer Henry
James and later of E F Benson, author
of the Mapp and Lucia Tales. Exhibits
include letters, pictures and furniture.

facilities: 🐕 ♿

Audley End House and Gardens

Audley End House and Gardens, Audley End,
CB11 4JF   **t:** (01799) 522842   **w:** english-heritage.org.uk

open: Gardens: Apr–Sep, Wed–Sun 1000–1800. Oct, Sat–Sun 1000–1700. Feb–Mar, Sat–Sun 1000–1500. House: Apr–Sep, Wed–Fri 1100–1600, Sat 1200–1400, Sun 1100–1600. Oct, Mar, Sat–Sun 1000–1500.

admission: £9.20

description: Visit a former wonder of the nation and experience the sumptuous splendour enjoyed by royalty and the aristocracy in one of England's grandest stately homes.

facilities:

Eastbury Manor House

Eastbury Manor House, Eastbury Square, Barking, IG11 9SN
t: (020) 8724 1002   **w:** barking-dagenham.gov.uk

open: Mon–Tue weekly, 1st & 2nd Sat of every month 1000–1600.

admission: £2.50

description: Grade II Listed manor in Barking, a magnificent venue for fairs, family days, evening events and medieval weekends. Gift shop, tea room and beautiful grounds. Public events throughout the year.

facilities:

Hedingham Castle

CASTLE HEDINGHAM

Hedingham Castle, Bayley Street, Castle Hedingham,
C09 3DJ **t:** (01787) 460261 **w:** hedinghamcastle.co.uk

open: Apr–Oct, Mon–Thu, Sun 1000–1700.
admission: £5.00

description: The finest Norman keep in England, built in 1140 by the de Veres, Earls of Oxford. Visited by Kings Henry VII and VIII and Queen Elizabeth I and besieged by King John.

facilities:

Hylands House

CHELMSFORD

Hylands House, Hylands Park, London Road, Chelmsford,
CM2 8WQ **t:** (01245) 605500
w: chelmsford.gov.uk/hylands

open: Apr, Mon 1100–1600, Sun 1100–1800.
May–Oct, Mon, Sun 1100–1800. Nov–Mar,
Mon 1100–1600, Sun 1100–1800.
admission: £3.40

description: Hylands House is a beautiful Grade II* Listed building, set in 574 acres of parkland.

facilities:

Colchester Castle

Colchester Castle, Castle Park, Colchester, CO1 1TJ
t: (01206) 282939   **w:** colchestermuseums.org.uk

open:	All year, Mon–Sat 1000–1700, Sun 1100–1700.
admission:	£5.00

description: A Norman keep on the foundations of a Roman temple. The archaeological material includes much on Roman Colchester (Camulodunum). Exciting hands-on displays.

facilities: 🍴 ♿

Hadleigh Castle

Hadleigh Castle, Hadleigh, SS7 2PP
t: (01223) 582700   **w:** english-heritage.org.uk

open: Daily.

description: Familiar from Constable's painting, the castle stands on a bluff overlooking the Leigh Marshes with a single, large 50ft tower and 13thC and 14thC remains.

facilities: 🍴 ⛱ ♿

Ingatestone Hall

Ingatestone Hall, Hall Lane, Ingatestone, CM4 9NR
t: (01277) 353010

open:	Apr–Jul, Sat–Sun, Bank Hols 1300–1800. Aug, Wed–Sun 1300–1800. Sep, Sat–Sun, Bank Hols 1300–1800.
admission:	£4.00

description: Tudor house and gardens, the home of the Petre family since 1540, with a family portrait collection, furniture and other heirlooms on display.

facilities:

Layer Marney Tower

Layer Marney Tower, Layer Marney, CO5 9US
t: (01206) 330784   **w:** layermarneytower.co.uk

open:	Apr–Sep, Mon–Thu, Sun 1200–1700.
admission:	£4.00

description: A 1520 Tudor-brick gatehouse, eight storeys high with Italianate terracotta cresting and windows. Gardens, park and rare breed farm animals and also the nearby church.

facilities:

Mountfitchet Castle

Mountfitchet Castle, Stansted Mountfitchet, CM24 8SP
t: (01279) 813237   **w:** mountfitchetcastle.com

open:	Mar–Nov, daily 1000–1700.
admission:	£6.50

description: A reconstructed Norman motte-and-bailey castle and village of the Domesday period with a Grand Hall, church, prison, siege tower and weapons. Domestic animals roam the site.

facilities:

Priors Hall Barn

Prior's Hall Barn, Widdington, CB11 3ZB
t: 0870 333 1181   **w:** english-heritage.org.uk

open: Apr–Sep, Sat,Sun 1000–1800.

description: One of the finest surviving medieval barns in south east England, representative of the type of aisled barn found in north west Essex. Superb aisled interior and crown post roof.

facilities:

Lodge Park & Sherborne Estate

ALDSWORTH

Lodge Park & Sherborne Estate, Aldsworth,
GL54 3PP   **t:** (01451) 844130   **w:** nationaltrust.org.uk

open:	Grandstand/Deer Park: Mar–Oct, Mon, Fri, Sun 1100–1600. Estate: All year, daily.
admission:	£4.50

description: Lodge Park is part of the Sherborne Estate, an ornate building dating from 1635, overlooking the deer course and surrounding countryside.

facilities:

Berkeley Castle

BERKELEY

Berkeley Castle, Berkeley, GL13 9BQ
t: (01453) 810332   **w:** berkeley-castle.com

open:	Apr–Sep, Tue–Sat, Bank Holiday Mon 1100–1600, Sun 1400–1700. Oct, Sun 1400–1700. Regular special events and concerts.
admission:	£7.50
description:	England's oldest inhabited castle. Over 24 generations the Berkeleys have transformed a savage Norman fortress into a stately home full of treasures. Learn about murder and intrigue, then enjoy the grounds and church.

facilities:

Pittville Pump Room

CHELTENHAM

Pittville Pump Room, Pittville Park, Cheltenham, GL52 3JE
t: (01242) 523852

open: All year, Mon, Wed–Sun 1000–1600.

description: Pittville Pump Room is a beautiful, historic Grade I Listed property set in parkland at Pittville used for cultural, commercial and community events.

facilities: 🐕 ⛱ ♿

Dyrham Park

DYRHAM

Dyrham Park, Dyrham, SN14 8ER
t: (0117) 937 2501 **w:** nationaltrust.org.uk

open: Park: Daily 1100–1700. House: Mar–Oct, Mon–Tue, Fri–Sun 1200–1700.
admission: £9.00

description: Mansion built between 1691 and 1710 for William Blathwayt. A herd of deer has roamed the 263-acre parkland since Saxon times.

facilities: 🍽 🐕 ⛱ ♿

Snowshill Manor (National Trust)

SNOWSHILL

Snowshill Manor (National Trust), Snowshill, WR12 7JU
t: (01386) 852410   **w:** nationaltrust.org.uk

open:	House: Apr–Oct, Wed–Sun 1200–1700.
	Gardens: Apr–Oct. Wed–Sun 1100–1730.
admission:	£7.30
description:	Cotswold manorhouse with eclectic collection of craftsmanship and arts and crafts garden.
facilities:	🍵 🏹 ♿

Sudeley Castle Gardens and Exhibition

WINCHCOMBE

Sudeley Castle Gardens and Exhibition, Winchcombe,
GL54 5JD   **t:** (01242) 602308   **w:** sudeleycastle.co.uk

open:	Apr–Oct, daily, Bank hols 1030–1700.
admission:	£7.20

description: Last home and burial place of Catherine Parr, with royal connections spanning the centuries. Seasonal exhibitions and award-winning organic gardens.

facilities: 🍵 🏹 🪑 ♿

Dunham Massey Hall Park and Garden (NT)

ALTRINCHAM

Dunham Massey Hall Park and Garden (National Trust),
Altrincham, WA14 4SJ   **t:** (0161) 941 1025
w: thenationaltrust.org.uk

open:	House: Apr–Oct, Mon–Wed, Sat–Sun 1200–1700. Park: Apr–Oct, Daily 0900–1930. Nov–Feb, Daily 0900–1700.
admission:	£6.50
description:	An 18thC mansion in a 250-acre wooded deer park with furniture, paintings and silver. Also, a 25-acre informal garden with mature trees and waterside plantings.
facilities:	■ 🎿 ⛱ ♿

Bramall Hall

BRAMHALL

Bramall Hall, Bramall Park, Bramhall, SK7 3NX
t: (0161) 485 3708
w: stockport.gov.uk/heritageattractions

open: Apr–Sep, Mon–Thu, Sun 1300–1700, Fri–Sat 1300–1600. Oct–Dec, Tue–Sun 1300–1600. Jan–Mar, Sat–Sun 1300–1600.
Bank Hols 1100–1700.

admission:	£3.95
description:	A Tudor manor house with 60 acres of landscaped grounds with lakes, woods and gardens. The house contains 16thC wall paintings. Tearoom and gift shop.
facilities:	■ 🎿 ⛱ ♿

Heaton Hall

MANCHESTER

Heaton Hall, Heaton Park, Prestwich, Manchester, M25 5SW
t: (0161) 773 1231   **w:** manchestergalleries.org

open:	Apr–Aug, Thu–Sun, Bank Hols 1100–1730.
description:	A magnificent 18thC country house set in Heaton Park's rolling landscape. Original features include beautiful scrolling plasterwork and classically inspired paintings.
facilities:	☕ ⚔ ♿

Breamore House

BREAMORE

Breamore House, Breamore, SP6 2DF
t: (01725) 512233   **w:** breamorehouse.com

open:	Apr, Tue, Sun 1400–1730. May–Sep, Tue–Thu, Sat–Sun, Bank Hols 1400–1730.
admission:	£7.00
description:	An Elizabethan manor house dating from 1583, with a fine collection of works of art. Furniture, tapestries, needlework, paintings (mainly Dutch School 17thC and 18thC).
facilities:	⚔ ♿

Jane Austen's House

Jane Austen's House, Chawton, GU34 1SD
t: (01420) 83262   **w:** jane-austens-house-museum.org.uk

open: 1 Jan–28 Feb, Sat–Sun 1000–1630. Mar–31 Dec, daily 1030–1630. Jun, Jul and Aug, daily 1000–1700
admission: £5.00

description: A 17thC house where Jane Austen lived from 1809-1817, and wrote or revised her six great novels. Letters, pictures, memorabilia, garden with old-fashioned flowers.

facilities: ⚹ ♿

Highclere Castle and Gardens

Highclere Castle and Gardens, Highclere, RG20 9RN
t: (01635) 253210   **w:** highclerecastle.co.uk

open: Apr, Jul–Aug, Mon–Thu, Sun, Bank Hols 1100–1630.
admission: £7.50

description: Highclere Castle is a splendid example of early Victorian architecture built in 1838-42. Home of the Earl of Carnarvon. Unique display of Egyptian antiquities.

facilities: 🍴 ⚹ ♿

Mottisfont Abbey Garden, House and Estate

MOTTISFONT

Mottisfont Abbey Garden, House and Estate, Mottisfont, SO51 0LP **t:** (01794) 340757 **w:** nationaltrust.org.uk

open: House: Apr–May, Sep–Oct, Mon–Wed, Sat–Sun, 1100–1700. Jun, daily 1100–1700. Jul, Mon–Thu, Sat–Sun 1100–1700. Garden: Apr–May, Sep–Oct, Mon–Wed, Sat–Sun 1100–1700. Jun, daily 1100–2030. Jul–Aug, Mon–Thu, Sat–Sun 1100–1700. Nov–Dec, Sat–Sun 1100–1600.

admission: £7.50

description: The garden, with the River Test flowing through it and its collection of old-fashioned roses, forms a superb setting for the 12thC priory.

facilities: ☕ 🐾 🛉 ♿

Portchester Castle

PORTCHESTER

Portchester Castle, Castle Street, Portchester, PO16 9QW   **t:** (023) 9237 8291
w: english-heritage.org.uk

open: Apr–Sep, daily 1000–1800. Oct–Mar, daily 1000–1600.

admission: £4.00

description: A Roman-Saxon shore fort with Norman additions. A near-perfect keep and Norman church within the walls. Spectacular views over the castle and Portsmouth.

facilities: 🐾 🛉 ♿

Broadlands

Broadlands, Romsey, SO51 9ZD
t: (01794) 505010   **w:** broadlands.net

open:	Jun–Sep, Mon–Fri, Bank Hols 1300–1730.
admission:	£8.00

description: One of the finest examples of mid-Georgian architecture in England and home of the late Lord Mountbatten. Magnificent 18thC house and contents. Mountbatten exhibition.

facilities: 🏹 🛆 ♿

Vyne

The Vyne, Vyne Road, Sherborne St John, RG24 9HL
t: (01256) 883858   **w:** nationaltrust.org.uk

open:	House: Apr–Oct, Mon–Wed 1300–1700. Sat–Sun 1100–1700. Grounds: Apr–Oct, Mon–Wed, Sat–Sun 1100–1700. Feb, Sat–Sun 1100–1700.
admission:	£8.00
description:	Original house dating back to Henry VIII's time. Extensively altered in mid 17thC. Tudor chapel, beautiful gardens and lake. Woodland walks.

facilities: 🍽 🏹 🛆 ♿

Stratfield Saye House

Stratfield Saye House, Stratfield Saye, RG7 2BZ
t: (01256) 882882   **w:** stratfield-saye.co.uk

open:	July, Mon–Fri 1130–1700, Sat–Sun 1030–1700.
admission:	£8.00
description:	Family home of the Dukes of Wellington since 1817. The house, the Wellington exhibition, the great Duke's funeral carriage, the grave of Copenhagen and state coach.
facilities:	🍴 🏃 ⛩ ♿

Great Hall

The Great Hall, The Castle, Winchester, SO23 8PJ
t: (01962) 846476
w: hants.gov.uk/discover/places/great-hall.html

open:	Apr–Oct, daily 1000–1700. Nov–Feb, daily 1000–1600.
admission:	£1.00
description:	Great Hall featuring 'King Arthur's Round Table' and 13thC herb garden named after Queen Eleanor. The Round Table has hung here for over 600 years
facilities:	🏃 ♿

Brockhampton Estate National Trust

Brockhampton Estate National Trust, Brockhampton Estate, Lower Brockhampton, Bringsty, WR6 5TB
t: (01885) 482077   **w:** nationaltrust.org.uk

open:	Apr–Sep, Wed–Sun 1200–1700. Oct, Wed–Sun 1200–1600.
admission:	£5.00
description:	Late-14thC moated manor house and detached half-timbered 15thC gatehouse; a rare example of this structure.
facilities:	⬛ 🏃 ♿

Eastnor Castle

Eastnor Castle, Eastnor, HR8 1RL
t: (01531) 633160   **w:** eastnorcastle.com

open:	Apr–Jul, Sun, Bank Hols 1100–1630. Aug, Mon–Fri, Sun 1100–1630. Sep, Sun, Bank Hols 1100–1630.
admission:	£7.50
description:	Fairytale Georgian castle, standing at the end of the Malvern Hills. A fine collection of armour, pictures, tapestries and Italian furniture.
facilities:	⬛ 🏃 ⛱ ♿

Goodrich Castle
(English Heritage)

GOODRICH

Goodrich Castle (English Heritage), Goodrich,
HR9 6HY   **t:** (01600) 890538   **w:** english-heritage.org.uk

open:	Mar–May, daily 1000–1700. Jun–Aug, daily 1000–1600. Sep–Oct, daily 1000–1700. Nov–Feb, Wed–Sun 1000–1600.
admission:	£4.90

description: Remarkably complete, magnificent red sandstone castle with 12thC keep and extensive remains from the 13thC and 14thC. Stunning views across the Wye Valley.

facilities: ☕ 🍴 ⛱ ♿

Old House

HEREFORD

The Old House, High Town, Hereford, HR1 2AA
t: (01432) 260694   **w:** herefordshire.gov.uk/leisure

open: Apr–Sep, Tue–Sat 1000–1700, Sun 1000–1600. Oct–Mar, Tue–Sat 1000–1700.

description: Built in 1621, with Jacobean domestic architecture, furnished in the17thC style, on three floors. The house includes kitchen and bedrooms originally part of Butchers Row.

facilities: 🍴 ⛱ ♿

Berrington Hall
(National Trust)

Berrington Hall (National Trust), Leominster, HR6 0DW
t: (01568) 615721   **w:** nationaltrust.org.uk

open: Apr–Nov, Mon–Wed, Sat–Sun 1300–1700.

admission: £6.00

description: Built in the late 18th century, designed by
Henry Holland. Beautifully decorated ceilings
and naval battle paintings. Grounds by
Capability Brown. Views of Welsh Hills.

facilities: 💻 ✕ 🏓 ♿

Croft Castle
(National Trust)

Croft Castle (National Trust), Leominster, HR6 9PW
t: (01586) 780246   **w:** nationaltrust.org.uk

open: Apr–Sep, Wed–Sun 1300–1700. Oct, Wed–Sun
1300–1600.

admission: £6.00

description: Property of the Croft family since Domesday,
with a break of 170 years from 1750. Original
walls and corner towers of 14thC, 15thC and
18thC Georgian Gothic staircase and ceiling.

facilities: 💻 ✕ 🏓 ♿

Shaw's Corner

Shaw's Corner, Ayot St Lawrence, AL6 9BX
t: (01438) 820307   w: nationaltrust.org.uk

open:	House: Apr–Oct, Wed–Sun 1300–1700. Garden: Apr–Oct, Wed–Sun 1200–1730.
admission:	£4.50

description: The home of George Bernard Shaw from 1906 until his death in 1950, with literary and personal effects on display and a 3.5-acre garden.

facilities: 🐾 🪑 ♿

Berkhamsted Castle

Berkhamsted Castle, Berkhamsted
t: (01536) 402840
w: english-heritage.org.uk

open: Apr–Oct, daily 1000–1800. Nov–Mar, daily 1000–1600.

description: The extensive remains of an 11thC motte-and-bailey castle which was the work of Robert of Mortain, half brother of William of Normandy, who learnt he was king here.

facilities: 🐕

Gorhambury

Gorhambury, Gorhambury, AL3 6AH
t: (01727) 855000

open:	May–Sep, Thu 1400–1700.
admission:	£6.00

description: A classical-style mansion built 1777-1784 by Sir Robert Taylor with 16thC enamelled glass, 17thC carpet and historic portraits of the Bacon and Grimston families.

facilities: ⚔ ♿

Hatfield House

Hatfield House, Hatfield, AL9 5NQ
t: (01707) 287010   **w:** hatfield-house.co.uk

open:	Apr–Sep, Wed–Sun, Bank Hols 1200–1700.
admission:	£9.00

description: Magnificent Jacobean house, home of the Marquess of Salisbury.

Exquisite gardens, model soldiers and park trails. Childhood home of Queen Elizabeth I.

facilities: ⚔ ♿

Knebworth House, Gardens and Park

Knebworth House, Gardens and Park, The Estate Office,
Knebworth House, Knebworth, SG3 6PY
t: (01438) 812661   **w:** knebworthhouse.com

open:	See website for details.
admission:	£9.00
description:	Tudor manor house, re-fashioned in the 19thC, housing a collection of manuscripts, portraits and Jacobean banquet hall. Formal gardens, parkland and adventure playground.
facilities:	▣ 夶 ㋡

Nunwell House

Nunwell House, Coach Lane, Brading, PO36 0JQ
t: (01983) 407240

open:	Jul–Sep, Mon–Wed 1300–1700.
admission:	£5.00
description:	Nunwell with its historic connections with Charles I is set in beautiful gardens and parkland with channel views. House has Jacobean and Georgian wings. Family military collection.
facilities:	夶 ㋻ ㋡

Osborne House

Osborne House, York Avenue, East Cowes, PO32 6JX
t: (01983) 200022   **w:** english-heritage.org.uk

open:	Apr–Sep, daily 1000–1800. Oct, daily 1000–1600. Nov–Mar, please phone for details.
admission:	£9.50

description: Queen Victoria and Prince Albert's seaside holiday home. Swiss Cottage where royal children learnt cooking and gardening. Victorian carriage rides. Award-winning gardens. New visitor centre with exhibition and shop.

facilities: ▬ ✗ ⊼ ♿

Carisbrooke Castle

Carisbrooke Castle, Castle Hill, Newport, PO30 1XY
t: (01983) 522107   **w:** english-heritage.org.uk

open:	Apr–Oct, daily 1000–1700. Nov–Mar, daily 1000–1600.
admission:	£5.60
description:	A splendid Norman castle, where Charles I was imprisoned. The governor's lodge houses the county museum. Wheelhouse with wheel operated by donkeys.

facilities: ▬ 🐕 ⊼ ♿

See pages 2-3 for key to symbols

Appuldurcombe House and Isle of Wight Falconry Centre

WROXALL

Appuldurcombe House and Isle of Wight Falconry Centre, Wroxall, PO38 3EW   **t:** (01983) 840188
w: appuldurcombe.co.uk

open:	Apr–Sep, daily 1000–1600.
admission:	£6.75

description: Ruins of 18thC house and garden. Park landscaped by Capability Brown. Front of house re-roofed and windows reglazed. Home of Isle of Wight Owl and Falconry Centre.

facilities:

Godinton House and Gardens

ASHFORD

Godinton House and Gardens, Godinton Lane, Ashford, TN23 3BP   **t:** (01233) 620773
w: godinton-house-gardens.co.uk

open:	Gardens: Apr–Oct, Mon, Thu–Sun 1400–1730. House: Apr–Oct, Fri–Sun 1400–1730.
admission:	£6.00

description: The house dates back to 1390 and has exquisite carving and a fine collection of furniture and porcelain. The famous yew hedge encloses contrasting gardens, from formal to wild.

facilities:

Deal Castle

Deal Castle, Victoria Road, Deal, CT14 7BA
t: (01304) 372762   **w:** english-heritage.org.uk

open:	Apr–Sep, Mon–Fri 1000–1800, Sat 1000–1700, Sun 1000–1800.
admission:	£4.00

description:	The largest of Henry VIII's coastal forts built c1540 with 119 gun positions. Tudor-rose shaped with outer moat. It also has a coastal-defence exhibition.

facilities:

Dover Castle and Secret Wartime Tunnels

Dover Castle and Secret Wartime Tunnels, Dover
Castle, Dover, CT16 1HU   **t:** (01304) 211067
w: english-heritage.org.uk

open:	All year, Mon, Thu–Sun 1000–1600.
admission:	£9.50

description:	One of the most powerful medieval fortresses in Western Europe. St Mary-in-Castro Saxon church, Roman lighthouse, secret wartime tunnels, Henry II Great Keep.

facilities:

Hever Castle and Gardens

Hever Castle and Gardens, Hever, TN8 7NG
t: (01732) 865224   **w:** hevercastle.co.uk

open: Grounds: Apr–Nov, daily 1100–1800. Castle: Apr–Nov, daily 1200–1800.

admission: £9.80

description: A moated castle once the childhood home of Anne Boleyn. Restored by the Astor family, it contains furniture, paintings and panelling. Set in award-winning gardens.

facilities: ⬛ 🐕 ⛱ ♿

Ightham Mote

Ightham Mote, Ivy Hatch, TN15 0NT
t: (01732) 811145   **w:** nationaltrust.org.uk

open: House: Apr–Oct, Mon, Wed–Fri, Sun 1030–1730. Garden: Apr–Oct, Mon, Wed–Fri, Sun 1000–1730. Estate: All year, dawn–dusk.

admission: £9.50

description: A medieval moated manor house with Great Hall, two chapels, 18thC drawing room and courtyard. Garden and woodland walk. Ongoing repair programme.

facilities: ⬛ ✂ ⛱ ♿

Leeds Castle
and Gardens

Leeds Castle and Gardens, Broomfield, Maidstone,
ME17 1PL   **t:** (01622) 765400   **w:** leeds-castle.com

open:	Gardens: Daily 1000–1700. Castle: Daily 1030–1600.
admission:	£13.50

description: A castle on two islands in a lake, dating from 9thC. Furniture, tapestries, art treasures, dog collar museum, gardens, duckery, aviaries, maze, grotto and vineyard.

facilities: ☕ ⚞ ⏃ ♿

Stoneacre

Stoneacre, Otham, ME15 8RS
t: (01622) 862871   **w:** nationaltrust.org.uk

open:	Apr–Sep, Sat 1100–1800.
admission:	£3.50

description: A small, attractive half-timbered manor house built mainly in the late 15thC. Visitors can see the Great Hall, crownpost and the newly-restored cottage-style garden.

facilities: ⚞ ♿

PENSHURST

Penshurst Place and Gardens

Penshurst Place and Gardens, Penshurst, TN11 8DG
t: (01892) 870307 **w:** penshurstplace.com

open: Gardens: Apr–Oct, daily 1030–1800. House: Apr–Oct, daily 1200–1600.
admission: £7.50

description: A medieval manor house with Baron's Hall, portraits, tapestries, armour, park, lake, venture playground, toy museum and with Tudor gardens. Gift shop.

facilities:

RICHBOROUGH

Richborough Roman Fort

Richborough Roman Fort, Richborough, CT13 9JW
t: (01304) 612013 **w:** english-heritage.org.uk

open: Apr–Sep, daily 1000–1800.
admission: £4.00

description: The ruins of a Roman fort and the landing place of the invasion of AD43. Fortified in the 3rdC and then improved by the Saxons.

facilities:

Restoration House

Restoration House, 17-19 Crow Lane, Rochester, ME1 1RF
t: (01634) 848520   **w:** restorationhouse.co.uk

open:	Jun–Sep, Thu–Fri 1000–1700.
admission:	£5.50

description:	An historic city mansion with a unique atmosphere and links to Charles II, Pepys and Dickens. There are beautiful interiors and a classic English garden.

facilities: ☕ ⚔ ⛩ ♿

Rochester Castle

Rochester Castle, The Keep, Rochester, ME1 1SX
t: (01634) 402276   **w:** medway.gov.uk

open:	Apr–Oct, daily 1000–1800. Nov–Mar, daily 1000–1600.
admission:	£4.00

description:	One of the finest and best-preserved keeps in England. Also the tallest, partly built on the Roman city wall. Views from the battlements over the River Medway.

facilities: ⚔ ⛩

Upnor Castle

Upnor Castle, High Street, Upper Upnor, Rochester,
ME2 4XG   **t:** (01634) 718742   **w:** medway.gov.uk/tourism

open:	1 Apr–30 Sep, Mon–Sun, Bank Hols 1000–1800. 1 Oct–31 Oct, Mon–Sun 1000–1600.
admission:	£4.50
description:	An Elizabethan artillery fort built 1559-1601 to protect the Royal Navy dockyards at Chatham. Displays on the 1667 battle against the Dutch and cannons from ships sunk in the battle.
facilities:	🐕 🪑

Knole

Knole, Sevenoaks, TN15 0RP
t: (01732) 462100   **w:** nationaltrust.org.uk

open:	House: Apr–Oct, Wed–Sun, Bank Hols 1200–1600. Garden: Apr–Oct, Wed, Bank Hols 1100–1600. Park: Daily.
admission:	£8.50
description:	One of England's 'Treasure Houses', dating from 1456. Important collections of portraits, silver, tapestries and unique 17thC Royal Stuart furniture. Set in deer park.
facilities:	☕ 🍴 ♿

Smallhythe Place

Smallhythe Place, Smallhythe, Tenterden, TN30 7NG
t: (01580) 762334   **w:** nationaltrust.org.uk

open:	Apr–Oct, Mon–Wed, Sat–Sun 1100–1700.
admission:	£5.00
description:	A 16thC house, home of actress Dame Ellen Terry containing personal and theatrical mementoes. Cottage grounds include her rose garden, orchard, nuttery and the Barn Theatre.
facilities:	☕ 🏹 ⛱ ♿

Belmont House and Gardens

Belmont House and Gardens, Belmont Park, Throwley,
ME13 0HH   **t:** (01795) 890202   **w:** belmont-house.org

open:	House: Apr–Sep, Sat–Sun, Bank Hols 1400–1700. Gardens: Daily 1000–dusk.
admission:	£6.00
description:	A late-18thC country mansion designed by Samuel Wyatt, seat of the Harris family since 1801. Harris clock collection, mementos of connections with India. Gardens and pinetum.
facilities:	☕ 🏹 ♿

Tonbridge Castle

Tonbridge Castle, Castle Street, Tonbridge, TN9 1BG
t: (01732) 770929   **w:** tonbridgecastle.org

open:	Apr–Sep, Mon–Fri 0900–1700, Sat 0900–1700, Sun 1030–1700. Oct–Mar, Mon–Fri 0900–1700, Sat 0900–1600, Sun 1030–1600.
admission:	£5.30

description: The remains of a Norman motte-and-bailey castle in grounds by the River Medway. A 13thC gatehouse with models, scenes and audiovisual effects depicts life at that time.

facilities:

Walmer Castle and Gardens

Walmer Castle and Gardens, Kingsdown Road, Walmer, CT14 7LJ   **t:** (01304) 364288
w: english-heritage.org.uk

open:	Apr–Sep, Mon–Fri 1000–1800, Sat 1000–1600, Sun 1000–1800. Oct, Wed–Sun 1000–1600. Mar, Wed–Sun 1000–1600.
admission:	£6.30

description: Walmer Castle is Tudor rose-shaped with a central tower and moat. It is the official residence of the Lord Warden of the Cinque Ports and contains contemporary Gardens.

facilities:

Chartwell

Chartwell, Mapleton Road, Westerham, TN16 1PS
t: (01732) 868381   **w:** nationaltrust.org.uk

open:	Apr–Jun, Sep–Oct, Wed–Sun 1100–1700. Jul–Aug, Thu–Sun 1100–1700.
admission:	£10.80

description: The home of Sir Winston Churchill with study, studio and museum rooms with gifts, uniforms and photos. Garden, Golden Rose walk, lakes and exhibition.

facilities: 　🍵 🐕 ⛩ ♿

Quebec House

Quebec House, Quebec Square, Westerham, TN16 1TD
t: (01732) 868381   **w:** nationaltrust.org.uk

open:	Apr–Oct, Wed–Sun, Bank Hols 1300–1630.
admission:	£3.90

description: A mostly 17thC red brick gabled house and the boyhood home of General Wolfe. Four rooms on view contain family photographs and prints. Exhibition on Battle of Quebec.

facilities: 　🚶 ♿

Squerryes Court Manor House and Gardens

WESTERHAM

Squerryes Court Manor House and Gardens, Westerham, TN16 1SJ   **t:** (01959) 562345
w: squerryes.co.uk

open:	Apr–Sep, Wed–Thu, Sun, Bank Hols 1130–1630.
admission:	£6.50
description:	Beautiful manor house, built 1681 containing tapestries, Old Master paintings, porcelain, furniture and items relating to General Wolfe. Gardens, lake, walks, and formal garden.
facilities:	

Gawthorpe Hall and Estate Block (NT)

BURNLEY

Gawthorpe Hall and Estate Block (National Trust), Burnley Road, Padiham, Burnley, BB12 8UA   **t:** (01282) 771004
w: lancsmuseums.gov.uk

open:	Apr–Oct, Tue–Thu, Sat–Sun 1300–1700.
admission:	£4.00
description:	The house was built in 1600 and restored by Sir Charles Barry in the 1850s. A loan from the National Portrait Gallery adds to the notable paintings already displayed.
facilities:	

Leighton Hall

Leighton Hall, Carnforth, LA5 9ST
t: (01524) 734474   **w:** leightonhall.co.uk

open: May–Jul, Tue–Fri, Bank Hols 1400–1700. Aug, Tue–Fri, Sun 1230–1700. Sep, Tue–Fri, Bank Hols 1400–1700.
admission: £6.00

description: The award-winning hall is the lived-in house of the famous furniture-making Gillow dynasty. Here, visitors can unravel the fascinating past of this ancient Lancashire family.

facilities: 🐕

Clitheroe Castle Museum

Clitheroe Castle Museum, Castle Hill, Castle Gate, Clitheroe, BB7 1BA   **t:** (01200) 424635   **w:** visitlancashire.com

open: Apr–Oct, Mon–Sat, Bank Hols 1115–1630, Sun 1300–1630. Nov, Sat 1115–1630, Sun 1300–1630.

admission: £2.20

description: The museum's displays cover a wide variety of topics including reconstructions of a Victorian kitchen, a printer's shop and a clogger's shop, birds of the Ribble Valley and local geology.

facilities: 🏃 ⛩ ♿

Lancaster Castle

Lancaster Castle, Shire Hall, Castle Parade, Lancaster,
LA1 1YJ   **t:** (01524) 64998   **w:** lancastercastle.com

open: All year, daily 1000–1700.
admission: £5.00

description: Shire Hall has a collection of coats of arms, a crown court, a grand jury room, a 'drop room' and dungeons. There is also an external tour of the castle.

facilities: 🏹 ♿

Rufford Old Hall

Rufford Old Hall, 200 Liverpool Road, Rufford, Ormskirk,
L40 1SG   **t:** (01704) 821254   **w:** nationaltrust.org.uk

open: Apr–Oct, Mon–Wed, Sat–Sun 1300–1700.
admission: £4.90

description: One of the finest 16thC buildings in Lancashire. The magnificent timber-framed Tudor hall, with impressive wood carvings, is believed to have hosted the young William Shakespeare.

facilities: ☕ 🏹

Hoghton Tower

Hoghton Tower, Hoghton, Preston, PR5 0SH
t: (01254) 852986   **w:** hoghtontower.co.uk

open:	Jul–Sep, Mon–Thu, Bank Hols 1100–1600, Sun 1300–1700.
admission:	£6.00
description:	A historic house with magnificent state apartments, banqueting hall, ballroom, grounds and dolls' houses on display. Underground passages and dungeons.
facilities:	🐕

Samlesbury Hall

Samlesbury Hall, Preston New Road, Samlesbury, Preston, PR5 0UP   **t:** (01254) 812229
w: samlesburyhall.co.uk

open:	All year, Mon–Fri, Sun 1100–1630.
admission:	£3.00
description:	A black and white, oak-timbered medieval manor house dating from 1325. The hall is home to displays, craft exhibitions and antique sales.
facilities:	🖥 🎿 ♿

Turton Tower TURTON

Turton Tower, Chapeltown Road, Turton, BL7 0HG
t: (01204) 852203 **w:** lancashire.com/lcc/museums

open:	Apr–May, Mon–Wed, Sat–Sun 1200–1600. Jun–Sep, Mon–Thu, Sat–Sun 1200–1700. Oct–Mar, Mon–Wed, Sat–Sun 1200–1600.

admission: £4.00

description: A medieval tower and Tudor country house, with 16thC Stuart and Victorian period rooms. The house features a collection of furniture from the Victoria and Albert Museum.

facilities: 🖥 🏹 ♿

Ashby-de-la-Zouch Castle ASHBY-DE-LA-ZOUCH

Ashby-de-la-Zouch Castle, South Street,
Ashby-de-la-Zouch, LE65 1BR
t: (01530) 413343 **w:** english-heritage.org.uk

open: Apr–Jun, Mon, Thu–Sun 1000–1700. Jul–Aug, daily 1000–1800. Sep–Oct, Mon, Thu–Sun 1000–1700. Nov–Mar, Mon, Thu–Sun 1000–1600.

admission: £3.50

description: The remains of a Norman manor house which Lord Hastings turned into a castle in the 15th century. Remains of a tower, parts of walls, great hall, private chambers, kitchen and chapel.

facilities: 🏹 ⛩ ♿

Belvoir Castle

Belvoir Castle, Estate Office, Belvoir, NG32 1PE
t: (01476) 871000   **w:** belvoircastle.com

open:	Apr, Sat–Sun 1100–1700. May–Jun, Tue–Thu, Sat–Sun 1100–1700. Jul–Aug, Mon–Thu, Sat–Sun 1100–1700. Sep, Sat–Sun 1100–1700.
admission:	£11.00

description: The fourth castle to have stood on the site since Norman times, completed in the early 19th century. Sloping lawns lead to the gardens which are elegantly laid out around a central fountain.

facilities: 🏇

Manor House

The Manor House, Manor Road, Donington le Heath, Coalville, LE67 2FW   **t:** (01530) 831259
w: leics.gov.uk/museums

open: Apr–Dec, daily 1100–1600.

description: A medieval manor house of the early 14thC with 16th-17thC alterations, oak furniture of the 16th-17thC, a herb garden and restaurant.

facilities: ☕ 🏇 ⛩ ♿

Stanford Hall

LUTTERWORTH

Stanford Hall, Stranford-upon-Avon, Lutterworth, LE17 6DH
t: (01788) 860250   **w:** stanfordhall.co.uk

open:	House: Apr–Sep, Sun, Bank Hols 1330–1730. Grounds: Apr–Sep, Sun, Bank Hols 1200–1730.
admission:	£6.00
description:	A William and Mary house on the River Avon with family costumes, furniture, pictures, a replica 1898 flying machine, rose garden and nature trail.
facilities:	■ ⚒ ♿

Belton House, Park and Gardens

BELTON

Belton House, Park and Gardens, Belton, NG32 2LS
t: (01476) 566116   **w:** nationaltrust.org.uk

open: House: Apr–Oct, Wed–Sun 1230–1700. Park: Apr–Jul, Wed–Sun 1100–170. Aug, daily 1030–1730. Sep–Oct, Wed–Sun 1100–1730. Garden: Apr–Jul, Wed–Sun 1100–1730. Aug, daily 1030–1730. Sep–Oct, Wed–Sun 1100–1730. Nov, Fri–Sun 1200–1600. Feb, Sat–Sun 1200–1600.
admission: £9.00

description:	The crowning achievement of restoration country house architecture, built 1685-1688 for Sir John Brownlow. Formal gardens, orangery and landscaped park.
facilities:	■ ⚒ ⛩ ♿

Gainsborough Old Hall

GAINSBOROUGH

Gainsborough Old Hall, Parnell Street, Gainsborough, DN21 2NB   **t:** (01427) 612669   **w:** lincolnshire.gov.uk

open: Apr–Oct, Mon–Sat 1000–1700, Sun 1300–1630. Nov–Mar, Mon–Sat 1000–1700.
admission: £3.80

description: Magnificent medieval manor house in the centre of Gainsborough with original kitchens, great hall and tower. Connections with Richard III, Henry VIII, The Mayflower Pilgrims and John Wesley. Regular exhibitions and events.

facilities:

Grimsthorpe Castle, Park and Gardens

GRIMSTHORPE

Grimsthorpe Castle, Park and Gardens, Estate Office, Grimsthorpe, PE10 0LY   **t:** (01778) 591205
w: grimsthorpe.co.uk

open: Castle: Apr–Jul, Sep, Thu, Sun, Bank Hols 1300–1700. Aug, Mon–Thu, Sat–Sun 1300–1700. Park: Apr–May, Thu, Sun, Bank Hols 1100–1800. Jun–Sep, Mon–Thu, Sat–Sun 1100–1800.
admission: £8.00

description: The castle covers four periods of architecture with a collection of portraits and furniture which are mainly 18thC.

facilities:

Doddington Hall

Doddington Hall & Gardens, Doddington, Lincoln,
LN6 4RU   t: (01522) 694308   w: doddingtonhall.com

open: Hall: May–Sep, Wed, Sun, Bank Hols 1300–1700. Gardens: May–Sep, Wed, Sun, Bank Hols 1200–1700.
admission: £5.60

description: Superb Elizabethan mansion by the renowned architect Robert Smythson, standing today as it was completed in 1600 with walled courtyards, turrets, gatehouse. 6 acres of romantic garden.

facilities:

Lincoln Castle

Lincoln Castle, Castle Hill, Lincoln, LN1 3AA
t: (01522) 511068   w: lincolnshire.gov.uk/lincolncastle

open: Apr–Oct, Mon–Sat 0930–1730, Sun 1100–1730. Nov–Mar, Mon–Sat 0930–1600, Sun 1100–1600.
admission: £3.80

description: Lincoln Castle is located in the heart of the historic City of Lincoln and is one of the county's leading tourist attractions.

facilities:

Bolingbroke Castle

OLD BOLINGBROKE

Bolingbroke Castle, Old Bolingbroke, PE23 4HJ
t: (01529) 461499 **w:** lincsheritage.org

open: All year, dawn–dusk.

description: A prime example of 13thC castle design complete with large gatehouse, round towers and moat. Only the ground floors of the towers and the lower parts of the walls remain.

facilities:

Burghley House

STAMFORD

Burghley House, Stamford, PE9 3JY
t: (01780) 752451 **w:** burghley.co.uk

open: Apr–Oct, Mon–Thu, Sat–Sun 1100–1700.
admission: £9.00

description: The largest and grandest house of the first Elizabethan age. Built between 1555 and 1587, it features fine paintings, tapestries, ceramics and works of art.

facilities:

Tattershall Castle

Tattershall Castle, Tattershall, LN4 4LR
t: (01526) 342543   **w:** nationaltrust.org.uk

open:	Apr–Sep, Mon–Wed, Sun 1100–1730, Sat 1300–1730. Oct, Mon–Wed, Sun 1100–1600, Sat 1300–1600. Nov, Sat, 1300–1600, Sun 1200–1600.
admission:	£4.50
description:	Tattershall Castle was built in the 15th century, to impress and dominate, by Ralph Cromwell, one of the most powerful men in England.
facilities:	▆ ⚒ ⊓ ♿

Hall Place and Gardens

Hall Place and Gardens, Hall Plac, Bourne Road, Bexley, DA5 1PQ   **t:** (01322) 526574   **w:** hallplaceandgardens.com

open: House: Apr–Oct, Mon–Sat 1000–1700, Sun, Bank Hols 1100–1700. Nov–Mar, Tue–Sat 1000–1615. Gardens: Daily, 0800–dusk.

description:	Tudor house and award-winning gardens built for the Lord Mayor of London in the reign of Henry VIII in 1537.
facilities:	▆ ⚒ ⊓ ♿

Syon House

Syon House, Syon Park, Brentford, TW8 8JF
t: (020) 8560 0881   **w:** syonpark.co.uk

open:	House: Apr–Oct, Wed–Thu. Sun, Bank Hols 1100–1700. Gardens: Mar–Oct, daily 1030–1700. Nov–Feb, Sat–Sun 1030–1600.
admission:	£8.00
description:	The house is set within 200 acres of Capability Brown-landscaped parkland and contains some of Robert Adam's finest interiors. The gardens incorporate the spectacular Great Conservatory and over 200 species of trees.
facilities:	▬ ✗ ⛤ ♿

Old Palace, Croydon

Old Palace, Croydon, Old Palace Road, Croydon, CR0 1AX
t: (020) 8256 1891   **w:** friendsofoldpalace.org

open:	See website for tour dates.
admission:	£7.00
description:	Fifteenth-century Great Hall, Great Chamber and chapel, Long Gallery, 13thC undercroft and the bedroom of Queen Elizabeth I.
facilities:	✗

Osterley Park House (NT)

Osterley Park House (National Trust), Jersey Road, Isleworth, TW7 4RB   **t:** (020) 8232 5050   **w:** nationaltrust.org.uk

open:	Apr–Oct, Wed–Sun 1300–1630.
admission:	£7.50

description: In 1761, the founders of Child's Bank commissioned Robert Adam to transform a crumbling Tudor mansion into an elegant neo-Classical villa. The spectacular interiors contain one of Britain's most complete examples of Adam's work.

facilities: 🕴 🏕 ♿

---

2 Willow Road

2 Willow Road, London, NW3 1TH
t: (020) 7435 6166   **w:** nationaltrust.org.uk

open:	Apr–Oct, Thu–Sat 1200–1700. Nov, Mar 1200–1700.
admission:	£4.40

description: Designed and built by Erno Goldfinger in 1939, it is one of Britain's most important examples of Modernist architecture and is filled with furniture also designed by Goldfinger.

facilities: 🕴 ♿

Buckingham Palace

Buckingham Palace, London, SW1A 1AA
t: (020) 7766 7300   **w:** royalcollection.org.uk

open:	Aug–Sep, daily 0945–1545.
admission:	£15.00

description: The official London
residence of the Queen.
Its 19 state rooms are
lavishly furnished with
some of the finest
treasures from the Royal Collection.

facilities: 🏃 ♿

Carlyle's House

Carlyle's House, 24 Cheyne Row, London, SW3 5HL
t: (020) 7352 7087   **w:** nationaltrust.org.uk

open:	Apr–Oct, Wed–Fri 1400–1700, Sat–Sun 1100–1700.
admission:	£4.50

description: This Queen Anne house was the home of
historian, social writer and ethical thinker
Thomas Carlyle and his wife Jane. The
furniture, pictures, portraits and books are all
still in place.

facilities: 🏃 ⛱ ♿

Chiswick House

Chiswick House, Burlington Lane, London, W4 2RP
t: (020) 8995 0508   **w:** english-heritage.org.uk

open:	Apr–Oct, Wed–Fri 1000–1700, Sat 1000–1400, Sun, Bank Hols 1000–1700.
admission:	£4.90

description: The celebrated villa of Lord Burlington with impressive grounds featuring Italianate garden with statues, temples, obelisks and urns.

facilities: ▣ ⚒ ⛼ ♿

Eltham Palace

Eltham Palace, Court Yard, London, SE9 5QE
t: (020) 8294 2548   **w:** english-heritage.org.uk

open:	Apr–Oct, Mon–Wed, Sun 1000–1700. Nov–Dec, Mon–Wed, Sun 1000–1600. Feb–Mar, Mon–Wed, Sun 1000–1600.
admission:	£7.60

description: A spectacular fusion of 1930s Art Deco villa and magnificent 15thC Great Hall. Surrounded by period gardens.

facilities: ▣ ⚒ ♿

Fenton House

Fenton House, Hampstead Grove, London, NW3 6SP
t: (020) 7435 3471   **w:** nationaltrust.org.uk

open:	Apr–Oct, Wed–Fri 1400–1700, Sat–Sun 1100–1700.
admission:	£5.50

description: A delightful 17thC merchant's house set among the winding streets of old Hampstead. The charming interior houses outstanding collections of Oriental and European porcelain, needlework, furniture and early keyboard instruments.

facilities: 🍴 ♿

Jewel Tower

Jewel Tower, Abingdon Street, Westminster, London, SW1P 3JY   **t:** (020) 7222 2219   **w:** english-heritage.org.uk

open:	Apr–Oct, daily 1000–1700. Nov–Mar, daily 1000–1600.
admission:	£2.90

description: One of only two original surviving buildings of the Palace of Westminster. Home today to 'Parliament Past and Present' - a fascinating account of the House of Lords and the House of Commons.

facilities: 🍴 ⛱ ♿

Kensington Palace State Apartments

Kensington Palace State Apartments, Kensington Gardens, London, W8 4PX   **t:** 0870 751 5170   **w:** hrp.org.uk

open:	Mar–Oct, daily 1000–1800. Nov–Feb, daily 1000–1700.
admission:	£11.50

description: Home to the Royal Ceremonial Dress Collection, which includes some of Queen Elizabeth II's dresses worn throughout her reign, as well as 14 of Diana, Princess of Wales' evening dresses.

facilities: ☕ ⚔ ⛩ ♿

Kenwood House

Kenwood House, Hampstead Lane, London, NW3 7JR   **t:** (020) 8348 1286
w: english-heritage.org.uk

open:	Apr–Oct, daily 1100–1700. Nov–Mar, daily 1100–1600.

description: A beautiful 18thC villa with fine interiors and a world-class collection of paintings. Also fabulous landscaped gardens and an award-winning restaurant.

facilities: ☕ ⚔ ⛩ ♿

Lauderdale House

LONDON

Lauderdale House, Waterlow Park, Highgate Hill, London, N6 5HG **t:** (020) 8348 8716 **w:** lauderdalehouse.co.uk

open: All year, Tue–Fri 1100–1600, Sat 1330–1700, Sun 1200–1700.

description: An old manor house built in 1582, situated in Waterlow Park. Community arts centre with a variety of concerts, children's shows, crafts and antiques fairs throughout the year.

facilities:

Old Royal Naval College

LONDON

Old Royal Naval College, Cutty Sark Gardens, Greenwich, London, SE10 9LW **t:** (020) 8269 4791
w: oldroyalnavalcollege.org

open: Daily 1000–1700.

description: In the heart of maritime Greenwich, the college is the site of the Greenwich Royal Hospital for Seamen, built to the designs of Christopher Wren, which later became the Royal Naval College.

facilities:

Queen's House

Queen's House, Romney Road, London, SE10 9NF
t: (020) 8858 4422   **w:** nmm.ac.uk

open: Daily 1000–1700.

description: The first Palladian-
style house in England
designed by Inigo Jones
for the Stuart queens
Anne of Denmark and
Henrietta Maria. The elegant interiors display
portraits/paintings of Greenwich and its naval
history.

facilities: 🚫🐕 ♿

Royal Hospital Chelsea

Royal Hospital Chelsea, Royal Hospital
Road, Chelsea, London, SW3 4SR
t: (020) 7881 5204

open: All year, Mon–Sat 1000–1200, 1400–1600.

description: Home of the Chelsea Pensioners, built by Sir
Christopher Wren between 1682 and 1690.
The chapel, Great Hall, Figure Court and
museum are of particular interest.

facilities: ☕ 🚫🐕 ♿

Somerset House

Somerset House, Strand, London, WC2R 1LA
t: (020) 7845 4670   **w:** somerset-house.org.uk

open:	Daily 1000–1800.
admission:	£5.00

description: A place for enjoyment, refreshment, arts and learning. This magnificent 18thC building houses the celebrated collections of the Courtauld Institute of Art Gallery, the Gilbert Collection and the Hermitage Rooms.

facilities: ⚐ ⊤ ♿

Spencer House

Spencer House, 27 St James's Place, London, SW1A 1NR
t: (020) 7499 8620   **w:** spencerhouse.co.uk

open:	Guided tours: Feb–Jul, Sep–Dec, Sun 1030–1745.
admission:	£9.00

description: Private palace built in 1756-66 for the first Earl Spencer, an ancestor of Diana, Princess of Wales. Eight state rooms furnished with antique and neo-classical furniture.

facilities: ⚐ ♿

Sutton House (NT)

Sutton House (National Trust), 2-4 Homerton High Street, London, E9 6JQ   **t:** (020) 8986 2264   **w:** nationaltrust.org.uk

open:	Feb–Dec, Thu–Sun 1230–1630.
admission:	£2.70

description:	Built in 1535, the house became home to successive merchants, Huguenot silk weavers, Victorian schoolmistresses and Edwardian clergy, and, although altered over the years, remains an essentially Tudor house.

facilities:

Rainham Hall

Rainham Hall, The Broadway, Rainham, RM13 9YN
t: (020) 7799 4552   **w:** nationaltrust.org.uk

open:	Apr–Oct, Sat, Bank Hols 1400–1700.
admission:	£2.50

description:	An attractive red-brick house, built in 1729, with stone dressing on symmetrical pattern. Exterior - brickwork and iron gates. Interior - trompe l'oeil paintwork.

facilities:

Ham House

Ham House, Ham Street, Ham, Richmond, TW10 7RS
t: (020) 8940 1950   **w:** nationaltrust.org.uk

open:	House: Apr–Oct, Mon–Wed, Sat–Sun 1300–1700. Garden: All year, Mon–Wed, Sat–Sun 1100–1800.
admission:	£9.00

description: The most complete survivor of 17thC fashion and power. Built in 1610 and enlarged in the 1670s, it was at the heart of Restoration court life and intrigue. Significant formal garden.

facilities: ☕ 🍴 🏕 ♿

Hampton Court Palace

Hampton Court Palace, Surrey, KT8 9AU
t: 0870 752 7777   **w:** hrp.org.uk

open:	Apr–Oct, daily 1000–1800. Nov–Mar, daily 1000–1630.
admission:	£12.30

description: Explore Henry VIII's state apartments, where history is brought to life with costumed guides. See the historic royal gardens and the world-famous maze - the oldest-surviving hedge maze still in use.

facilities: ☕ 🍴 🏕 ♿

Marble Hill House

Marble Hill House, Richmond Road, Twickenham, TW1 2NL
t: (020) 8892 5115   **w:** english-heritage.org.uk

open: Apr–Oct, Sat 1000–1400, Sun 1000–1700.
admission: £4.20

 **description:** A Palladian villa built for Henrietta Howard, mistress of King George II, set in 66 acres of parkland. The villa's intimate interiors give you a fascinating glimpse into Henrietta's lifestyle.

facilities:

Croxteth Hall and Country Park

Croxteth Hall and Country Park, Croxteth Hall Lane, Muirhead Avenue, Liverpool, L12 0HB
t: (0151) 228 5311   **w:** croxteth.co.uk

open: See website for details.

description: An Edwardian stately home set in 500 acres of countryside (woodlands and pasture), featuring a Victorian walled garden and animal collection.

facilities:

Speke Hall, Gardens and Woodland (NT)

Speke Hall, Gardens and Woodland (National Trust),
The Walk, Liverpool, L24 1XD
t: (0151) 427 7231   **w:** nationaltrust.org.uk

open:	See website for details.
admission:	£6.50

description:	A wonderful, rambling Tudor mansion with rich Victorian interiors, set in a wooded estate on the banks of the Mersey with views of Wirral and North Wales.

facilities:

Sudley House

Sudley House, Mossley Hill Road, Aigburth, Liverpool,
L18 8BX   **t:** (0151) 724 3245   **w:** sudleyhouse.org.uk

open:	Daily 1000–1700.

description:	A beautiful Victorian house and gardens situated in the Mossley Hill area of Liverpool, featuring George Holt's fine collection of paintings including works by Gainsborough, Reynolds, Landseer and Turner.

facilities:

Blickling Hall

Blickling Hall, Blickling, NR11 6NF
t: (01263) 738030   **w:** nationaltrust.org.uk

open: Apr–Jun, Wed–Sun 1300–1700. Jul–Aug, Mon, Wed–Sun 1300–1700. Sep–Oct, Wed–Sun 1300–1700.
admission: £8.50

description: A Jacobean redbrick mansion with garden, orangery, parkland and lake. Spectacular long gallery, plasterwork ceilings and fine collections of furniture, pictures, books & walks.

facilities:

Castle Acre Castle

Castle Acre Castle, Castle Acre, PE32 2AF
t: (01760) 755394   **w:** english-heritage.org.uk

open: Daily 0900–dusk.

description: The remains of a Norman manor house which became a castle with earthworks, set by the side of a village.

facilities:

Castle Rising Castle

Castle Rising Castle, Castle Rising, PE31 6AH
t: (01553) 631330   **w:** english-heritage.org.uk

open: Apr–Sep, daily 1000–1800. Nov–Mar, Wed–Sun 1000–1600.

admission: £3.85

description: Castle Rising Castle is a fine example of a Norman castle. The rectangular keep, one of the largest, was built around 1140 by William D'Albini.

facilities: 🐕 ♿

Felbrigg Hall

Felbrigg Hall, Felbrigg, NR11 8PR
t: (01263) 837444   **w:** nationaltrust.org.uk

open: Apr–Oct, Mon–Wed, Sat–Sun 1300–1700.

admission: £7.50

description: A 17thC country house with original 18thC furniture and pictures. There is also a walled  garden, orangery, park and woodland with waymarked walks, shops and catering.

facilities: 🍴 🐕 ⛱

Houghton Hall

Houghton Hall, Houghton, PE31 6UE
t: (01485) 528569   **w:** houghtonhall.com

open:	Apr–Sep, Wed–Thu, Sun, Bank Hols 1330–1700.
admission:	£8.00
description:	Built in the 18thC with superb staterooms. Five-acre walled garden provides colour all summer. Unique collection of 20,000 model soldiers. Restaurant, shop and picnic area.
facilities:	

Dragon Hall

Dragon Hall, 115-123 King Street, Norwich, NR1 1QE
t: (01603) 663922   **w:** dragonhall.org

open:	Mar–Dec, Mon–Fri 1000–1700, Sun 1100–1600.
admission:	£5.00
description:	Medieval merchant's hall with outstanding timber-framed structure. The 15thC Great Hall has a crown-post roof with an intricately carved and painted dragon.
facilities:	

Norwich Castle

NORWICH

Norwich Castle, Shirehall, Market Avenue, Norwich,
NR1 3JQ   **t:** (01603) 493625
w: museums.norfolk.gov.uk

open: Term Time: Mon–Fri 1000–1630, Sat
1000–1700, Sun 1300–1700. School Hols:
Mon–Sat 1000–1730, Sun 1300–1700.
admission: £4.30

description: The ancient Norman keep of Norwich Castle
dominates the city and is one of the most
important buildings of its kind in Europe.

facilities:

Oxburgh Hall

OXBOROUGH

Oxburgh Hall, Oxborough, PE33 9PS
t: (01366) 328258   **w:** nationaltrust.org.uk

open: Apr–Jul, Mon–Wed, Sat–Sun 1300–1700. Aug,
daily 1300–1700. Sep, Mon–Wed, Sat–Sun
1300–1700. Oct, Mon–Wed, Sat–Sun 1300–
1600.
admission: £6.75

description: A 15thC moated redbrick
fortified manor house
with an 80ft gatehouse,
Mary Queen of Scot's
needlework, a Catholic

priest's hole, garden, woodland walks and a
Catholic chapel.

facilities:

Sandringham

Sandringham, Sandringham, PE35 6EN
t: (01553) 612908   **w:** sandringhamestate.co.uk

open:	House: Apr–Oct, daily 1100–1645. Museum: daily 1100–1700. Gardens: daily 1030–1700.
admission:	£9.00
description:	The country retreat of HM The Queen. A delightful house set in 60 acres of gardens and lakes. There is also a museum of royal vehicles and royal memorabilia.
facilities:	

Holkham Hall

Holkham Hall, Wells-next-the-Sea, NR23 1AB
t: (01328) 710227

open:	Jun–Sep, Mon–Thu, Sun 1200–1700.
admission:	£7.00
description:	A classic 18thC Palladian-style mansion. Part of a great agricultural estate and a living treasure house of artistic and architectural history along with a bygones collection.
facilities:	

Duncombe Park

Duncombe Park, Helmsley, YO62 5EB
t: (01439) 770213   w: duncombepark.com

open: Gardens: May–Oct, Mon–Thu, Sun 1100–1730. House: May–Oct, Mon–Thu, Sun 1230–1530.
admission: £2.00

description: A magnificent family home, owned and restored by Lord and Lady Feversham. The original 18thC house was remodelled after a serious fire in the late 19th century.

facilities: 🍽 🐕 🪑 ♿

Helmsley Castle

Helmsley Castle, Helmsley, YO62 5AB   t: (01904) 601974
w: english-heritage.org.uk/yorkshire

open: See website for details.
admission: £4.00

description: Helmsley Castle has been in existence for over 900 years. Originally a medieval castle, a Tudor mansion was added in the 1600s before Cromwell's men blew up the great keep.

facilities: 🐕 🪑 ♿

Hovingham Hall

HOVINGHAM

Hovingham Hall, Hovingham, YO62 4LU
t: (01653) 628771 **w:** hovingham.co.uk

open: Jun, Mon–Sat 1315–1630.
admission: £6.00

description: An outstanding example of Palladian architecture, designed c1760 by Thomas Worsley. The hall looks out onto the famous private cricket ground, where most of the greatest Yorkshire cricketers have played.

facilities:

Sion Hill Hall

KIRBY WISKE

Sion Hill Hall, Kirby Wiske, YO7 4EU
t: (01845) 587206 **w:** sionhillhall.co.uk

open: Jun–Sep, Wed 1300–1700.
admission: £4.50

description: The hall was designed in 1912 by the renowned York architect Walter H Brierley, 'The Lutyens of the North', and was designated by the Royal Institute of British Architects.

facilities:

Bolton Castle

Bolton Castle, Leyburn, DL8 4ET
t: (01969) 623981   **w:** boltoncastle.co.uk

open:	Apr–Sep, daily 1000–1700. Oct–Mar, daily 1000–1600.
admission:	£5.00
description:	Fortress with nine-foot-thick walls which has dominated Wensleydale since 1379. Mary Queen of Scots was imprisoned here during 1568 and 1569 and the Royalists were besieged here during the Civil War.
facilities:	☕ 🍴 ⌠

Middleham Castle (EH)

Middleham Castle (English Heritage), Middleham, DL8 4QR
t: (01904) 601974   **w:** english-heritage.org.uk

open:	See website for details.
admission:	£3.50
description:	The castle was the childhood and favourite home of Richard III. The massive  keep, one of the largest in England, served as a defensive building and self-contained residence.
facilities:	🐕 ⌠

Allerton Park

Allerton Castle, Nr
Knaresborough, HG5 0SE
t: (01423) 330927
w: allertoncastle.co.uk

open:	Easter–Sep, Wed 1300–1700.
admission:	£6.50

description: Most elegant of the surviving Gothic Revival country houses, massive guest hall, elegant carved wood rooms. Mechanical music machine collection.

facilities: 🖥 🐕 🪑

Nunnington Hall

Nunnington Hall, Nunnington, YO62 5UY
t: (01439) 798340   **w:** nationaltrust.org.uk

open:	Apr–May, Tue–Sun 1200–1600. Jun–Aug, Tue–Sun 1200–1730. Sep–Oct, Tue–Sun 1200–1700.
admission:	£5.20

description: Large 17thC manor house situated on the banks of River Rye. Hall, bedrooms, nursery, maid's room (haunted), Carlisle collection of miniature rooms and National Trust shop.

facilities: 🖥 🍴 🪑 ♿

Pickering Castle (EH)

Pickering Castle (English Heritage), Pickering, YO18 7AX
t: (01904) 601974   **w:** english-heritage.org.uk

open:	See website for details.
admission:	£3.00

description: Originally built by William the Conqueror to suppress the rebellious northerners, this castle was used by a succession of medieval kings as a hunting lodge, holiday home and stud farm.

facilities: 🐕 ⛱ ♿

Richmond Castle

Richmond Castle, Richmond, DL10 4QW
t: (01904) 601974   **w:** english-heritage.org.uk

open:	See website for details.
admission:	£3.60

description: Built shortly after the Battle of Hastings, this is the best-preserved castle of such scale and age in the country and alleged to be where the legendary King Arthur lies sleeping.

facilities: 🐕 ⛱ ♿

Ripley Castle

RIPLEY

Ripley Castle, Ripley, HG3 3AY
t: (01423) 770152 **w:** ripleycastle.co.uk

open: Castle: Apr–Oct, daily 1100–1500. Nov, Tue, Thu, Sat–Sun 1100–1500. Dec–Feb, Sat–Sun 1100–1500. Mar, Tue–Thu, Sat–Sun 1100–1500. Gardens: Apr–Oct, daily 0900–1700. Nov–Feb 0900–1630.

admission: £7.00

description: Ripley Castle, home to the Ingilby family for over 26 generations, is set in the heart of a delightful estate with Victorian walled gardens, deer park and pleasure grounds.

facilities:

Newby Hall & Gardens

RIPON

Newby Hall & Gardens, Ripon, HG4 5AE
t: 0845 450 4068 **w:** newbyhall.com

open: House; Apr–Jun, Tue–Sun1200–1700. Jul–Aug, daily 1200–1700. Sep, Tue–Sun 1200–1700. Gardens; Apr–Jun, Tue–Sun 1100–1730. Jul–Aug, daily 1100–1730. Sep, Tue–Sun 1100–1730.

admission: £9.50

description: One of England's renowned Adam houses, an exceptional example of 18thC interior decoration. Contents include unique Gobelins tapestry room, classical statuary and fine Chippendale furniture.

facilities:

Scarborough Castle (EH)

Scarborough Castle (English Heritage),
Castle Road, Scarborough, YO11 1HY
t: (01904) 601974
w: english-heritage.org.uk

open: See website for details.
admission: £3.50

description: This 12thC castle is set high on the cliff tops and conceals over 2,500 years of turbulent history. It played a key role in national events up to the 20th century.

facilities:

Skipton Castle

Skipton Castle, Skipton, BD23 1AW
t: (01756) 792442   **w:** skiptoncastle.co.uk

open: Mar–Sep, Mon–Sat 1000–1800, Sun 1200–1800. Oct–Feb, Mon–Sat 1000–1600, Sun 1200–1600 (excl 25 Dec).

admission: £5.60

description: One of the most complete medieval castles in England with over 900 years of turbulent history. Picnic areas, licensed tea rooms,  shop with a notable book section, plant sales.

facilities:

Sutton Park

Sutton Park, Sutton-on-the-Forest, YO61 1DP
t: (01347) 810249   **w:** statelyhome.co.uk

open:	Apr–Sep, daily 1100–1700.
admission:	£3.50

description: Georgian stately home with fine furniture, magnificent plasterwork by Cortese and paintings from Buckingham House, now Buckingham Palace. Important collection of porcelain. Wonderful award-winning gardens.

facilities:

Beningbrough Hall & Gardens (NT)

Beningbrough Hall & Gardens (National Trust), Beningbrough, York, YO30 1DD   **t:** (01904) 470666   **w:** nationaltrust.org.uk

open: House: Jun, Mon–Wed, Sat–Sun 1200–1700. Jul–Aug, Mon–Wed, Fri–Sun 1200–1700. Sep–Oct, Mon–Wed, Sat–Sun 1200–1700. Grounds: Mar–June, Sep–Oct, Mon–Wed, Sat–Sun 1100–1730. Jul–Aug, Mon–Wed, Fri–Sun 1100–1730. Nov, Jan–Feb Sat–Sun 1100–1530.

admission: £7.00

description: Handsome Baroque house, built in 1716, housing 100 portraits from the National Portrait Gallery. The attraction also includes a restored walled garden.

facilities:

Castle Howard

Castle Howard, York, YO60 7DA
t: (01653) 648444   **w:** castlehoward.co.uk

open:	Grounds: daily 1000–dusk. House: Mar–Oct, daily 1100–1600.
admission:	£10.00

description: Home to the Howard family since 1699. Extensive collections, breathtaking parkland, outdoor tours, historical-character guides, archaeological dig, exhibition wing and events programme. Cafe, gift shop.

facilities: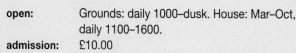

Fairfax House

Fairfax House, Castlegate, York, YO1 9RN
t: (01904) 655543   **w:** fairfaxhouse.co.uk

open:	All year, Mon–Thu, Sat 0900–1700, Sun 1330–1700.
admission:	£5.00
description:	Fairfax House is one of the finest 18thC townhouses in England, richly decorated within. Home to the famous Noel Terry collection of furniture and clocks.

facilities:

Treasurer's House (NT)

YORK

Treasurer's House (National Trust), Minster Yard, York, YO1 7JL **t:** (01904) 624247 **w:** nationaltrust.org.uk

open:	Apr–Oct, Mon–Thu, Sat–Sun 1100–1630. Nov, Mon–Thu, Sat–Sun 1100–1500.
admission:	£5.00
description:	Nestled behind the minster, this elegant house was carefully restored by wealthy local Victorian industrialist Frank Green, and contains 16thC-20thC decoration, furniture, china and glass.
facilities:	

Althorp

ALTHORP

Althorp, The Stables, Althorp, NN7 4HQ
t: (01604) 770107 **w:** althorp.com

open:	Jul–Aug, daily 1100–1700.
admission:	£12.00
description:	Built by Sir John Spencer in 1508 and altered by Henry Holland in 1790, with fine pictures, porcelain and furniture. The home of Earl Spencer and his family.
facilities:	

Canons Ashby House

CANONS ASHBY

Canons Ashby House, Canons Ashby, NN11 3SD
t: (01327) 861901 **w:** nationaltrust.org.uk

open: House: Apr–Sep, Mon–Wed, Sat–Sun 1300–1730. Oct–Nov, Mon–Wed, Sat–Sun 1300–1630. Dec, Sat–Sun 1200–1600. Church and Park: Apr–Sep, Mon–Wed, Sat-Sun 1100–1730. Oct–Nov, Mon–Wed, Sat–Sun 1100–1630. Dec, Sat–Sun 1100–1600. Gardens: Apr–Sep, Mon–Wed, Sat–Sun
admission: £7.00

description: The home of the Dryden family since its construction, this Elizabethan manor house has remained largely unaltered since 1710. Gardens, parkland, church, tearoom and shop.

facilities:

Cottesbrooke Hall and Gardens

COTTESBROOKE

Cottesbrooke Hall and Gardens, Cottesbrooke, NN6 8PF
t: (01604) 505808 **w:** cottesbrookehall.co.uk

open: May–Jun, Wed–Thu 1400–1730. Jul–Sep, Thu, Bank Hols 1400–1730.
admission: £7.50

description: A magnificent Queen Anne house dating from 1702, set in delightful rural Northamptonshire. It is reputed to be the pattern for Jane Austen's Mansfield Park.

facilities:

See pages 2-3 for key to symbols

Kirby Hall

Kirby Hall, Deene, NN17 1AA
t: (01536) 203230   **w:** english-heritage.org.uk

open:	Apr–Jun, Mon, Thu–Sun 1000–1700. Jul–Aug, daily 1000–1800. Sep–Oct, Mon, Thu–Sun 1000–1700. Nov–Mar, Mon, Thu–Sun 1000–1600.
admission:	£4.50
description:	Kirby Hall is one of the great Elizabethan houses, built in the hope of receiving the Queen on her annual 'progresses' round the country.
facilities:	🐕 ⛱ ♿

Holdenby House Gardens & Falconry Centre

Holdenby House Gardens & Falconry Centre, Holdenby House, Holdenby, NN6 8DJ   **t:** (01604) 770074
w: holdenby.com

open:	Gardens and Falconry: Apr, Sun 1300–1700. May–Aug, Sun, Bank Hols 1300–1700. Sep, Sun 1300–1700.
admission:	£5.00
description:	Holdenby's royal connections go back over 400 years. Built by Sir Christopher Hatton to entertain Elizabeth I, later the Palace of James I and the prison of his son, Charles I.
facilities:	🍽 ✗ ⛱ ♿

Kelmarsh Hall and Gardens

KELMARSH

Kelmarsh Hall and Gardens, Estate Office, Kelmarsh Hall,
Kelmarsh, NN6 9LY **t:** (01604) 686543 **w:** kelmarsh.com

open:	House: Apr–Sep, Thu, Bank Hols 1400–1700. Gardens: Apr–Sep, Tue–Thu, Sun, Bank Hols 1400–1700.
admission:	£5.00
description:	Built 1732 to a James Gibbs design, Kelmarsh Hall is surrounded by its working estate, grazed parkland and beautiful gardens. Successive owners and influences have left their imprint on the Palladian house and gardens.
facilities:	▬ ⋔ 冄 ⅙

Boughton House

KETTERING

Boughton House, Kettering, NN14 1BJ
t: (01536) 515731 **w:** boughtonhouse.org.uk

open:	May–Jul, Mon–Fri, Sun 1300–1700. Aug, Mon–Fri, Sun 1400–1700.
admission:	£7.00
description:	Northamptonshire home of The Duke of Buccleuch and his Montagu ancestors since 1528. A 500-year-old Tudor monastic building, gradually enlarged until the French-style addition of 1695.
facilities:	▬ ⋔ 冄 ⅙

78 Derngate

78 Derngate, 82 Derngate, Northampton, NN1 1UH
t: (01604) 603408   **w:** 78derngate.org.uk

open:	Apr–Oct, Wed–Sun, Bank Hols. Please phone for details.
admission:	£5.50
description:	Charles Rennie Mackintosh transformed a typical terraced house into a startlingly modern house with a striking interior. The adjoining property houses an exhibition about the original design.
facilities:	⚔

Southwick Hall

Southwick Hall, Oundle, PE8 5BL
t: (01832) 274064   **w:** southwickhall.co.uk

open:	All year, Bank Hols 1400–1700.
admission:	£5.00
description:	A manor house dating from the 14th century with Elizabethan and Georgian additions and an exhibition of Victorian and Edwardian costumes and country bygones.

facilities:	⚔ ♿

Rockingham Castle

ROCKINGHAM

Rockingham Castle, Rockingham, LE16 8TH
t: (01536) 770240   **w:** rockinghamcastle.com

open:	Apr–May, Sun, Bank Hols 1200–1700.
	Jun–Sep, Tue, Sun, Bank Hols 1200–1700.
admission:	£7.50

description: An Elizabethan house within the walls of a Norman castle, with fine pictures, extensive views and gardens with roses and an ancient yew hedge.

facilities: ▬ ⚔ 🛆 ♿

Rushton Triangular Lodge

RUSHTON

Rushton Triangular Lodge, Rushton, NN14 1RP
t: (01536) 710761   **w:** english-heritage.org.uk

open:	Apr–Oct, Mon, Thu–Sun 1000–1700.
admission:	£2.40

description: Completed by Sir Thomas Tresham in 1597 to symbolise the Trinity, with three sides, three floors and trefoil windows, and reputed meeting place of the Gunpowder Plot conspirators.

facilities: ⚔ 🛆 ♿

Sulgrave Manor

Sulgrave Manor, Manor Road, Sulgrave, OX17 2SD
t: (01295) 760205   **w:** sulgravemanor.org.uk

open:	Apr, Sat–Sun 1200–1600. May–Oct, Tue–Thu 1400–1600, Sat–Sun 1200–1600.
admission:	£5.75

description: An early English home of the ancestors of George Washington, with Washington souvenirs. A good example of a small manor house of Shakespeare's time with furniture of the period and kitchen.

facilities:

Alnwick Castle

Alnwick Castle, Alnwick Castle Ventures, Estates Office, Alnwick, NE66 1NQ   **t:** (01665) 510777
w: alnwickcastle.com

open:	Apr–Oct 1000–1800.
admission:	£9.00

description: One of Europe's finest medieval castles. Glorious state rooms, fine art and architecture, fascinating exhibitions, children's activities, special events, unique Knights Quest interactive games area. Best Large Attraction 2006 - North East Tourism Awards.

facilities:

Chillingham Castle

ALNWICK

Chillingham Castle, Chillingham, Alnwick, NE66 5NJ
t: (01668) 215359   **w:** chillingham-castle.com

open:	Castle: Apr–Sep, Mon–Fri, Sun 1300–1700.
	Grounds: Apr–Sep, Mon–Fri, Sun 1200–1700.
admission:	£6.75

description: Medieval fortress with Tudor additions. Torture chamber, shop, dungeon, tearoom, woodland walks, beautifully furnished rooms and Italian topiary garden with spectacular herbaceous borders.

facilities:

Bamburgh Castle

BAMBURGH

Bamburgh Castle, Bamburgh, NE69 7DF   **t:** (01668) 214515   **w:** bamburghcastle.com

open:	Apr–Oct, daily 1000–1700.
admission:	£6.50

description: Magnificent coastal castle completely restored in 1900 housing collections of china, porcelain, furniture, paintings, arms and armour. The castle is home to the Armstrong family.

facilities:

Belsay Hall, Castle and Gardens

Belsay Hall, Castle and Gardens, Belsay, NE20 0DX
t: (01661) 881636   **w:** english-heritage.org.uk

open:	See website for details.
admission:	£5.50

description:	Home of the Middleton family for 600 years. Thirty acres of landscaped gardens and winter garden. Fourteenth-century castle, ruined 17thC manor house and neoclassical hall.

facilities: ▆ ⵜ 丼 ♿

Berwick Castle

Berwick Castle, The Walls, Berwick-upon-Tweed, TD15 1HP
t: (01289) 304493   **w:** english-heritage.org.uk

open:	See website for details.
admission:	£3.40

description:	West wall of 12thC castle with 16thC gun tower which survived as a boundary for the railway yard, and late 13thC curtain wall descending to the river.

facilities: ⵜ ♿

Chipchase Castle

CHILLINGHAM

Chipchase Castle, Wark, Chillingham, NE48 3NT
t: (01434) 230203

open: Jun, daily 1400–1700.
admission: £5.00

description: One of the best examples of Jacobean architecture in the Borders. Chapel, 14thC pele tower, walled vegetable garden, wild garden with lake, nursery garden selling plants.

facilities: ☕ 🐕 ♿

Aydon Castle

CORBRIDGE

Aydon Castle, Corbridge, NE45 5PJ
t: (01434) 632450 **w:** english-heritage.org.uk

open: See website for details.
admission: £3.40

description: Fine example of a small castle built as a manor house in the late 13th century and fortified shortly after. It was converted to a farmhouse in the 17th century.

facilities: ♿

See pages 2-3 for key to symbols

Dunstanburgh Castle

CRASTER

Dunstanburgh Castle, Craster, NE66 3TT
t: (01665) 576231   **w:** english-heritage.org.uk

open:	See website for details.
admission:	£2.70

description: Romantic ruins of extensive 14thC castle in dramatic coastal situation on 100ft cliffs. Built by Thomas, Earl of Lancaster. Remains include gatehouse and curtain wall.

facilities: 🐕 ⛱

Edlingham Castle

EDLINGHAM

Edlingham Castle, Edlingham, NE66 2BL
t: (01289) 304493   **w:** english-heritage.org.uk

open: Daily dawn–dusk.

description: In a remote and picturesque valley, this complex ruined castle comprises a 13thC hall and house, a 14thC courtyard and a domestic tower added in the 15thC.

facilities: 🐕

Etal Castle

Etal Castle, Etal Village, Etal, TD12 4TN
t: (01890) 820332   **w:** english-heritage.org.uk

open: Apr–Oct, daily 1100–1600.
admission: £3.40

description: Typical compact 14thC border castle comprising four-storey keep, gatehouse, parts of curtain wall and corner tower. The 19thC chapel displays an award-winning exhibition.

facilities: 🏇 🎪 ♿

Cragside House, Gardens and Estate

Cragside House, Gardens and Estate, Cragside, Rothbury, Morpeth, NE65 7PX   **t:** (01669) 620333
w: nationaltrust.org.uk

open: House: Apr–Sep, Tue–Sun 1300–1730. Oct, Tue–Sun 1300–1630. Gardens: Apr–Oct, Tue–Sun 1030–1730. Nov, Wed–Sun 1100–1600.
admission: £11.55

description: The creation of Lord Armstrong, Cragside is a garden of breathtaking drama, whatever the season. This magnificent estate provides one of the last shelters for the endangered red squirrel.

facilities: ☕ 🏇 🎪 ♿

Norham Castle

Norham Castle, Norham, TD15 1DF
t: (01289) 382329   **w:** english-heritage.org.uk

open:	Apr–Sep, Sun, Bank Hols 1000–1700.
description:	One of the strongest of Border castles and one of the finest Norman keeps in England. The most famous siege in Sir Walter Scott's Marmion.
facilities:	犬 ㅠ 占

Warkworth Castle

Warkworth Castle, Warkworth, NE65 0UJ
t: (01665) 711423   **w:** english-heritage.org.uk

open:	See website for details.
admission:	£3.40
description:	Dramatic ruins dating from the 12thC-14thC, owned by the Percy family for 600 years. Remains include the 15thC keep, chapel, great hall and lion tower with carved lion.
facilities:	犬 占

Seaton Delaval Hall

WHITLEY BAY

Seaton Delaval Hall, Seaton Sluice, Whitley Bay, NE26 4QR
t: (0191) 237 1493

open:	Jun–Sep, Wed, Sun 1400–1800.
admission:	£4.00
description:	A splendid English baroque house comprising a centre block between two arcaded and pedimented wings. The east wing contains fine stables, and there are gardens with statues.
facilities:	

Newstead Abbey

RAVENSHEAD

Newstead Abbey, Newstead Abbey Park, Ravenshead,
NG15 8NA   **t:** (01623) 455900

open:	Park: All year, daily 0900–dusk. Abbey: Apr–Sep, daily 1200–1700.
admission:	£3.00
description:	The 800-year-old remains of a priory church, converted into a country house in the 16th century; the home of Lord Byron with possessions, manuscripts, parkland, a lake and gardens.
facilities:	

Buscot Park

Buscot Park, Buscot, SN7 8BU
t: (01367) 240786   **w:** buscot-park.com

open: Apr–Sep, see website for details.
admission: £7.00

description: An 18thC Palladian-style house with park and water garden. Home of the Faringdon collection of paintings and furniture. The park is landscaped with extensive water gardens.

facilities:

Kelmscott Manor

Kelmscott Manor, Kelmscott, GL7 3HJ
t: (01367) 252486   **w:** kelmscottmanor.co.uk

open: See website for details.
admission: £8.50

description: The country home of William Morris 1871-1896. The house contains a collection of the works of Morris and his associates, including furniture, textiles, carpets and ceramics.

facilities:

Mapledurham House

Mapledurham House, The Estate Office, Mapledurham,
RG4 7TR   **t:** (0118) 972 3350   **w:** mapledurham.co.uk

open:	Apr–Sep, Sat–Sun, Bank Hols 1400–1700.
admission:	£6.50

description:	An Elizabethan manor house alongside the River Thames, containing paintings, oak staircases, and moulded ceilings. Home to the Blount family for over 500 years.

facilities:

Nuffield Place

Nuffield Place, Nettlebed, RG9 5RY
t: (01491) 641224   **w:** nuffield-place.com

open:	Please see website for details.
admission:	£4.00

description:	Home and gardens of Lord Nuffield, founder of Morris Motors and benefactor to medicine, education and social welfare. Set high in the Chilterns. A day out for all the family.

facilities:

Blenheim Palace

Blenheim Palace, Woodstock, OX20 1PX
t: (01993) 811091   **w:** blenheimpalace.com

open:	Palace and Gardens: Feb–Oct, daily 1030–1730. Nov–9 Dec, Wed–Sun 1030–1730. Park: All year, daily 0900–1645.
admission:	£16.00

description: World Heritage site set in 2,100 acres of parkland landscaped by Capability Brown. Home to 11th Duke of Marlborough and the birthplace of Winston Churchill. Interiors feature superb carving, hand-painted ceilings and renowned collections.

facilities: ■ 🏃 🏓 ♿

Lyddington Bede House

Lyddington Bede House, Blue Coat Lane, Uppingham, LE15 9LZ   **t:** (01572) 822438   **w:** english-heritage.org.uk

open:	Apr–Oct, Mon, Thu–Sun 1000–1700.
admission:	£3.30
description:	The only surviving part of a medieval palace belonging to the Bishops of Lincoln, converted to almshouses in 1600 with an elaborate 16thC timber ceiling cornice on the first floor.

facilities: ■ 🏃 🏓 ♿

Dudmaston Hall

Dudmaston Hall, Quatt, Bridgnorth, WV15 6QN
t: (01746) 782821   **w:** nationaltrust.org.uk

open:	House: Apr–Sep, Tue–Wed, Sun 1400–1730. Grounds: Apr–Sep, Mon–Wed, Sun 1200–1800.
admission:	£5.80
description:	Dudmaston is a 17th C mansion with art collection, lakeside garden and estate.
facilities:	

Stokesay Castle

Stokesay Castle, Stokesay, Craven Arms, SY7 9AH
t: (01588) 672544
w: english-heritage.org.uk/stokesaycastle

open:	Mar–Apr, Wed–Sun 1000–1700. May–Jun, daily 1000–1700. Jul–Aug, daily 1000–1800. Sep–Oct, Wed–Sun 1000–1700. Nov–Feb, Thu–Sun 1000–1600.
admission:	£4.90
description:	The castle is the finest and best-preserved 13thC manor house in England, nestling in peaceful South Shropshire countryside near the Welsh border.
facilities:	

Ludlow Castle

Ludlow Castle, Castle Square, Ludlow, SY8 1AY
t: (01584) 873355   **w:** ludlowcastle.com

open:	Apr–Jul, daily 1000–1700. Aug, daily 1000–1900. Sep, daily 1000–1700. Oct–Dec, daily 1000–1600.
admission:	£4.00
description:	The construction of Ludlow Castle began in the late 11th century as the border stronghold of one of the Marcher Lords, Roger De Lacy.
facilities:	▆ ⊁ � ⴜ

Attingham Park

Attingham Park, Atcham, Shrewsbury, SY4 4TP
t: (01743) 708123   **w:** nationaltrust.org.uk

open:	House: Apr–Oct, Mon–Tue, Fri–Sat 1300–1730. Grounds: Apr–Oct, daily 1000–1730. Nov–Feb, daily 0900–1600.
admission:	£7.00
description:	For a meagre sum you may have the house and grounds to enjoy for a whole day. You'll see a late 18thC house commanding views over 500 acres of wonderful parkland.
facilities:	▆ ⊁ ㄷ ⴜ

Darby Houses (Ironbridge)

TELFORD

Darby Houses (Ironbridge), Darby Rd, Coalbrookdale,
Telford, TF8 7DQ   **t:** (01952) 435900
w: ironbridge.org.uk

open: Apr–Oct, daily 1000–1700.
admission: £3.50

description: In the Darby houses,
Dale House and Rosehill
House, you can delve into
the everyday life of Quaker
families.

facilities: ☆ ⊼ ♿

Assembly Rooms

BATH

Assembly Rooms, Bennett Street, Bath, BA1 2QH
t: (01225) 477789   **w:** museumofcostume.co.uk

open: Mar–Oct, daily, Bank Hols 1100–1700.
admission: £6.75

description: Designed by John
Wood the Younger in 1769. One of
Bath's finest Georgian buildings.
Includes Museum of Costume.

facilities: ☕ ☆ ♿

Pump Room

Pump Room, Abbey Church Yard, Bath, BA1 1LZ
t: (01225) 477785   **w:** romanbaths.co.uk

open:	Mar–Jun, daily 0900–1800. Jul–Aug, daily 0900–2100. Sep–Oct daily 0900–1800. Nov–Feb, daily 0930–1730.
admission:	£10.25
description:	With its elegant interior of c1795, the Pump Room is the social heart of Bath. Stop for refreshments or lunch and sample a glass of spa water from the fountain.
facilities:	☕ ✗

Clevedon Court

Clevedon Court, Tickenham Road, Clevedon, BS21 6QU
t: (01275) 872257   **w:** nationaltrust.org.uk

open:	Apr–Sep, Wed, Thu, Sun 1400–1700.
admission:	£5.80

description: Home of the Elton family. A 14thC manor-house, once partly fortified. Terraced garden with rare shrubs. Collection of  Nailsea glass and Eltonware. No photography allowed in house.

facilities: ☕ ✗ ♿

Dunster Castle

Dunster Castle, Dunster, TA24 6SL
t: (01643) 821314   **w:** nationaltrust.org.uk

open:	Apr–Jul, Mon–Wed, Fri–Sun 1100–1600. Aug, Mon–Wed, Fri–Sun 1100–1700. Sep–Oct, Mon–Wed, Fri–Sun 1100–1600.
admission:	£7.50
description:	Fortified home of the Luttrells for 600 years, remodelled 100 years ago. Fine 17thC staircase, plaster ceilings and garden of rare shrubs.
facilities:	⚔ 🎪 ♿

Montacute House

Montacute House, Montacute, TA15 6XP
t: (01935) 823289   **w:** nationaltrust.org.uk

open:	Apr–Oct, Mon, Wed–Sun 1100–1700.
admission:	£8.00

description: Late 16thC house built of local golden hamstone, by Sir Edward Phelips. The Long Gallery houses a collection of Tudor and Jacobean portraits. Formal gardens. Park.

facilities: 🍽 ⚔ 🎪 ♿

Cothay Manor

Cothay Manor, Greenham, Wellington, TA21 0JR
t: (01823) 672283
w: visitourgardens.co.uk/gardens/cothay.htm

open:	Apr–Sep, Wed–Thu, Sun, Bank Hols 1400–1800.
admission:	£4.50

description: Hidden for centuries, and virtually untouched since it was built in 1480. Said to be the finest example of a small classic medieval manorhouse remaining today.

facilities:

Bishop's Palace

The Bishop's Palace & Gardens, Wells, BA5 2PD   **t:** (01749) 678691
w: bishopspalacewells.co.uk

open:	Apr–Oct, Mon–Fri 1030–1800, Sun 1200–1800.
admission:	£5.00

description: Medieval palace and gardens surrounded by a moat and fortified walls.

facilities:

BRODSWORTH

Brodsworth Hall and Gardens

Brodsworth Hall and Gardens, Brodsworth Hall, Brodsworth, DN5 7XJ   **t:** (01904) 601974
w: english-heritage.org.uk

open: See website for details.
admission: £6.60

description: One of the most complete surviving examples of an English Victorian country house set in 15 acres of formal and informal gardens and woodland.

facilities: ⬛ 🏃 ⛩ ♿

HIMLEY

Himley Hall & Park

Himley Hall & Park, Himley, DY3 4DF
t: (01384) 817817   **w:** dudley.gov.uk

open: Park: Daily, dawn–dusk. Hall: Apr–Aug,
                   Tue–Sun, Bank Hols 1400–1700.

description: Historic house offering an excellent
                   programme of temporary exhibitions during
                   the spring and summer months and outdoor
                   events throughout the year.

facilities: ⬛ 🏃 ⛩ ♿

Complete Working Historic Estate of Shugborough (National Trust)

The Complete Working Historic Estate of Shugborough
(The National Trust), Shugborough, Milford, ST17 0XB
t: (01889) 881388   **w:** shugborough.org.uk

open:	Apr–Oct, daily 1000–1700.
admission:	£10.00
description:	Eighteenth-century mansion house with fine collection of furniture. Gardens and park contain beautiful neo-classical monuments.
facilities:	

Ford Green Hall

Ford Green Hall, Ford Green Road, Smallthorne,
ST6 1NG   **t:** (01782) 233195   **w:** stoke.gov.uk

open:	All year, Mon–Thu, Sun 1300–1700.
admission:	£2.50
description:	A 17thC timber-framed farmhouse with 18thC additions. Fully furnished with items from the 17th and 18thC.

facilities:	

Stafford Castle and Visitor Centre

Stafford Castle and Visitor Centre, Castle Bank, Newport Road, Stafford, ST16 1DJ   **t:** (01785) 257698
w: staffordbc.gov.uk

open: Apr–Oct, Tue–Sun 1000–1700. Nov–Mar, Sat–Sun 1000–1600.

description: On the site of one of the earliest castles, a typical example of a Norman fortress. Field work has revealed a deserted village site.

facilities: 🏃 🛆 ♿

Tamworth Castle

Tamworth Castle, The Holloway, Tamworth, B79 7NA
t: (01827) 709626   **w:** tamworth.gov.uk

open: All year, Thu–Sun 1200–1715.
admission: £4.95

description: Enter a world of history, magic and ghosts! Dramatic Norman castle with 15 rooms to explore. Free quizzes and lots of hands-on activities for children.

facilities: 🏃 ♿

Bungay Castle

BUNGAY

Bungay Castle, Bungay
t: (01986) 896156

open: Apr, Mon–Sat 1000–1600. May–Nov, daily 1000–1600. Dec–Mar, Mon–Sat 1000–1600.

description: The remains of an original Norman castle with Saxon mounds. Built by the Bigods in 1165. Massive gatehouse towers and curtain walls. Visitor centre with cafe.

facilities:

Bridge Cottage

EAST BERGHOLT

Bridge Cottage, Flatford, East Bergholt, CO7 6UL
t: (01206) 298260 **w:** nationaltrust.org.uk

open: Apr–Sep, daily 1030–1730. Oct–Dec, Wed–Sun 1100–1530. Jan–Feb, Sat–Sun 1100–1530. Mar, Wed–Sun 1100–1700.

description: A 16thC thatched cottage , just upstream from Flatford Mill, and housing an exhibition on landscape painter John Constable. Tearoom, shop, information centre & guided walks.

facilities:

See pages 2-3 for key to symbols

EYE

Eye Castle

Eye Castle, Castle Street, Eye
t: (01449) 676800

open: Apr–Oct, daily 0900–dusk.

description: A Norman motte-and-bailey with medieval walls and a Victorian folly. The castle has always had close associations with royalty since the Norman conquest.

facilities: 🐕 ♿

FRAMLINGHAM

Framlingham Castle

Framlingham Castle, Framlingham, IP13 9BP
t: (01728) 724189   **w:** english-heritage.org.uk

open: See website for details.
admission: £4.50

description: A magnificent castle, the home of Mary Tudor in 1553, with 12thC curtain walls, 13 towers, Tudor brick chimneys and a wall walk.

facilities: 🐕 ♿

Ickworth House, Park and Gardens

Ickworth House, Park and Gardens,
The Rotunda, Horringer, IP29 5QE
t: (01284) 735270   **w:** nationaltrust.org.uk

open:	House: Apr–Sep, Mon–Tue, Fri–Sun 1300–1700. Oct–Nov, Mon–Tue, Fri–Sun 1300–1630. Gardens: Apr–Sep, Mon–Tue, Fri–Sun 1000–1700. Oct–Feb, Mon–Tue, Fri–Sun 1100–1600. Park: Daily, 0800–2000.
admission:	£7.50
description:	An extraordinary oval house with flanking wings, begun in 1795. Fine paintings, a beautiful collection of Georgian silver, an Italian garden and stunning parkland.
facilities:	🖥 ⚰ 卅 ♿

Ipswich Unitarian Meeting House

The Ipswich Unitarian Meeting House, Friars Street, Ipswich,
IP1 1TD   **t:** (01473) 218217

open:	May–Sep, Tue, Thu 1200–1600. Sun 1000–1600.
description:	A Grade I Listed building, built 1699, opened in 1700. One of the finest surviving meeting houses and one of the most important historic structures in Ipswich.
facilities:	⚰ ♿

Little Hall

Little Hall, Market Place, Lavenham, CO10 9QZ
t: (01787) 247179

open:	Apr–Oct, Wed–Thu, Sat–Sun 1400–1730, Bank Hols 1100–1730.
admission:	£2.50
description:	A 14thC hall house with a crown-post roof which contains the Gayer-Anderson collection of furniture, pictures, sculpture and ceramics. There is also a small walled garden.
facilities:	🥾 ♿

Melford Hall

Melford Hall, Long Melford, CO10 9AA
t: (01787) 379228   **w:** nationaltrust.org.uk

open: Apr, Sat–Sun 1330–1700. May–Sep, Wed–Sun 1330–1700. Oct, Sat–Sun 1330–1700.
admission: £5.50

description:	Turreted brick Tudor mansion with connections to Beatrix Potter. Collection of Chinese porcelain, gardens and a walk in the grounds. Dogs on leads, where permitted.
facilities:	☕ 🐕 ♿

Orford Castle

Orford Castle, Orford, IP12 2ND
t: (01394) 450472   **w:** english-heritage.org.uk

open:	Apr–Sep, daily 1000–1800. Nov–Mar, Mon, Thu–Sun 1000–1600.
admission:	£4.70
description:	A 90ft-high polygonal keep with views across the River Alde to Orford Ness, built by Henry II for coastal defence in the 12thC.
facilities:	⚐ ⛱

Somerleyton Hall and Gardens

Somerleyton Hall and Gardens, Somerleyton,
NR32 5QQ   **t:** (01502) 730224   **w:** somerleyton.co.uk

open: Hall: Apr–Jun, Thu, Sun, Bank Hols 1200–1600. Jul–Aug, Tue–Thu, Sun 1200–1600. Sep–Oct, Thu, Sun, Bank Hols 1200–1600. Gardens: Apr–Jun, Thu, Sun, Bank Hols 1000–1700. Jul–Aug, Tue–Thu, Sun 1000–1700. Sep–Oct, Thu, Sun, Bank Hols 1000–1700.
admission: £7.50

description: Early Victorian stately mansion in Anglo-Italian style, with lavish features and fine state rooms. Beautiful 12-acre gardens, with historic yew hedge maze, gift shop.

facilities: ⚐ ♿

Gainsborough's House

Gainsborough's House, 46 Gainsborough Street,
Sudbury, CO10 2EU   **t:** (01787) 372958
w: gainsborough.org

open:	All year, Mon–Sat 1000–1700.
admission:	£4.00

description: The birthplace of Thomas Gainsborough. An elegant townhouse with paintings by the artist, a garden, print workshop and a programme of temporary exhibitions.

facilities: ⚹ ⊓ ♿

Euston Hall

Euston Hall, Euston Estate Office, Thetford, IP24 2QP
t: (01842) 766366   **w:** eustonhall.co.uk

open:	Jun–Sep, Thu 1430–1700.
admission:	£6.00

description: Hall housing paintings by Van Dyck, Lely and Stubbs, with pleasure grounds designed by John Evelyn and Capability Brown, and the 17thC Church of St Genevieve.

facilities: 🍴 ⚹ ⊓ ♿ᴾ

Hatchlands Park

Hatchlands Park, East Clandon, GU4 7RT
t: (01483) 222482   **w:** nationaltrust.org.uk

open:	Park: Apr–Oct, daily 1100–1800. House: Apr–Jul, Sep–Oct, Tue–Thu, Sun 1400–1730. Aug, Tue–Fri, Sun 1400–1730.
admission:	£6.60
description:	Built in 1758 and set in a Repton park, Hatchlands has splendid interiors by Robert Adam and houses the Cobbe collection of keyboard musical instruments. Jekyll Garden.
facilities:	▣ ᚁ 兲 ♿

Farnham Castle

Farnham Castle, The Castle, Farnham, GU9 0AG
t: (01252) 721194   **w:** farnhamcastle.com

open:	Guided tours of Bishop's Palace: All year, Wed 1400–1600. Apr–Aug, Fri 1430. Keep: Easter, May Bank Hols, Jun–Sep, Fri–Sun 1300–1700.
admission:	£2.50
description:	The former residence of the Bishops of Winchester and Guildford, Farnham Castle dates from Norman times. It has a chapel, great hall, Tudor brick tower and Gibbons carvings.
facilities:	ᚁ ♿

Polesden Lacey

Polesden Lacey, Great Bookham, RH5 6BD
t: (01372) 458203   **w:** nationaltrust.org.uk

open: House: Apr–Oct, Wed–Sun 1100–1700. Gardens: Apr–Oct, daily 1100–1700. Nov–Feb, daily 1100–1600.
admission: £6.50

description: A Regency villa, re-modelled after 1906 with collections of paintings, porcelain, tapestries and furniture. Walled rose garden, extensive grounds with landscape walks and woodland.

facilities: ♨ ⚒ ⏁ ♿

Guildford Castle

Guildford Castle, Castle Street, Guildford, GU1 3TU
t: (01483) 444750   **w:** guildfordmuseum.co.uk

open: Apr–Sep, daily 1000–1700. Oct, Mar, Sat–Sun 1100–1700. Oct half–term, daily 1100–1700.
admission: £2.20

description: An 11thC motte and bailey castle founded by William the Conqueror and extended by Henry III. The ruined keep

dominates the old town and was re-opened in June 2004 after extensive restoration.

facilities: ⚒ ⏁ ♿

Titsey Place and Gardens

Titsey Place and Gardens, Titsey Place, Oxted, RH8 0SD
t: (01273) 407056   **w:** titsey.org

open:	May–Sep, Wed, Sun, Bank Hols 1300–1700.
admission:	£5.00

description: A guided tour of Titsey Place includes the library, old servants' hall, dining room and drawing room. The gardens comprise 10 acres of formal gardens and a walled garden.

facilities:

Clandon Park

Clandon Park, West Clandon, GU4 7RQ
t: (01483) 222482   **w:** nationaltrust.org.uk

open:	House: Apr–Oct, Tue–Thu, Sun 1100–1630.
	Garden: Apr–Oct, Tue–Thu, Sun 1100–1700.
	Museum: Apr–Oct, Tue–Thu, Sun 1200–1700.
admission:	£7.20

description: A Palladian-style house built for Lord Onslow c1730. Marble hall, Gubbay collection of furniture, needlework and porcelain, Royal Surrey Regiment Museum, parterre in garden.

facilities:

Sir William Turner Alms Houses

Sir William Turner Alms Houses, 1 Sir William Turner's Court, Kirkleatham, TS10 4QT   **t:** (01642) 482828
w: communigate.co.uk/ne/swthospital

open: Group bookings only, please phone for details.
admission: £1.50

description: Founded in 1676 as
Almshouses for the poor. They
have been lived in continuously
to this day. Fine Georgian
chapel containing various
historical items.

facilities: ⚡ 𝕏 ⛩ ♿

Ormesby Hall

Ormesby Hall, Church Lane, Ormesby, Middlesbrough,
TS7 9AS   **t:** (01642) 324188   **w:** nationaltrust.org.uk

open: Apr–Nov, Sat–Sun 1330–1700.
admission: £4.40

description: Beautiful 18thC
mansion with park, gardens,
tearoom, impressive contemporary
plasterwork, magnificent stable
block attributed to Carr of York and
model railway exhibition and layout.

facilities: 💺 𝕏 ⛩ ♿

Tynemouth Castle and Priory

Tynemouth Castle and Priory, Tynemouth, NE30 4BZ
t: (0191) 257 1090   **w:** english-heritage.org.uk

open:	See website for details.
admission:	£3.40

description:	Dating from the 7th century, the burial place of Northumbrian kings. The priory was destroyed by the Danes, later founded as a Benedictine Priory, and is now a picturesque ruin.

facilities: 🐕 🪑 ♿

Washington Old Hall

Washington Old Hall, The Avenue, Washington Village,
Washington, NE38 7LE   **t:** (0191) 416 6879
w: nationaltrust.org.uk

open:	House: Apr–Oct, Mon–Wed, Sun 1100–1700. Gardens: Apr–Oct, Mon–Wed, Sun 1000–1700.
admission:	£4.40

description:	A delightful stone-built manor house on the site of the home of the ancestors of George Washington. Displays, gardens and 17thC room recreations. A gem of a property!

facilities: 🍽 ⚔ 🪑 ♿

Upton House

Upton House, Banbury, OX15 6HT
t: (01295) 670266   **w:** nationaltrust.org.uk

open:	Mar–Oct, Mon–Wed, Sat–Sun 1200–1700. Nov, Sat–Sun 1200–1600.
admission:	£8.00
description:	A late-17thC house, remodelled from 1927-1929 for the 2nd Viscount Bearsted, containing his internationally important collection of paintings and porcelain. Spectacular garden.
facilities:	

Kenilworth Castle

Kenilworth Castle, Castle Green, Kenilworth, CV8 1NE
t: (01926) 852078   **w:** english-heritage.org.uk

open: Apr–May, daily 1000–1700. Jun–Aug, daily 1000–1800. Sep–Oct, daily 1000–1700. Nov–Feb, daily 1000–1600. Mar, daily 1000–1700.
admission: £6.00

description:	Edward II signed his abdication here, John of Gaunt created the banqueting hall, and Elizabeth I was entertained by Robert Dudley.
facilities:	

Baddesley Clinton (National Trust)

Baddesley Clinton (National Trust), Rising Lane,
Baddesley Clinton, Knowle, B93 0DQ
t: (01564) 783294   **w:** nationaltrust.org.uk

open:	House: Apr, Wed–Sun 1330–1700. May–Sep, Wed–Sun 1330–1730. Oct, Wed–Sun 1330–1700. Grounds: Apr, Wed–Sun 1200–1700. May–Sep, Wed–Sun 1200–1730. Oct, Wed–Sun 1200–1700. Nov, Wed–Sun 1200–1600.
admission:	£8.00

description:	A medieval moated manor house with 120 acres, dating back to the 14thC. Little changed since 1634. Due to popularity, visits are timed.

facilities: ▬ 💺 ⚔ 🔆 ♿

Packwood House

Packwood House, Packwood Lane, Lapworth,
B94 6AT   **t:** (01564) 783294   **w:** nationaltrust.org.uk

open:	Mar–Oct, Wed–Sun 1200–1630.
admission:	£7.00

description:	Built in about 1560, a timber-framed house, substantially renovated in the early 1900s, containing a wealth of tapestries and furniture.

facilities: ⚔ 🔆 ♿

Arbury Hall

NUNEATON

Arbury Hall, Nuneaton, CV10 7PT
t: (024) 7638 2804

open: Hall: Easter–Aug Bank Hols, Sun, Mon 1400–1700. Gardens: Easter–Aug Bank Hols, Sun, Mon, 1330–1800.

admission: £6.50

description: Elizabethan building gothicised by Sir Roger Newdigate during the second half of the 18th century. Magnificent ceilings in Georgian plaster and landscaped gardens.

facilities:

Anne Hathaway's Cottage

SHOTTERY

Anne Hathaway's Cottage, Cottage Lane, Shottery, CV37 9HH **t:** (01789) 292100 **w:** shakepeare.org.uk

open: Apr–May, Mon–Sat 0930–1700, Sun 1000–1700. Jun–Aug, Mon–Sat 0900–1700, Sun 0930–1700. Sep–Oct, Mon–Sat 0930–1700, Sun 1000–1700. Nov—Mar, daily 1000–1600.

admission: £5.50

description: This world famous thatched cottage is the childhood home of Anne Hathaway, Shakespeare's wife, and remained in the Hathaway family until the 19th century.

facilities:

Nash's House & New Place

STRATFORD-UPON-AVON

Nash's House & New Place, Chapel Street, Stratford-upon-Avon, CV37 6EP   **t:** (01789) 292325   **w:** shakespeare.org.uk

open:	Apr–May, daily 1100–1700. Jun–Aug, Mon–Sat 0930–1700, Sun 1000–1700. Sep–Oct, daily 1100–1700. Nov–Mar, daily 1000–1600.
admission:	£3.75

description: The site of Shakespeare's last home, including an Elizabethan-style knot garden. Nash's House contains fine period furniture. Also, a museum of local history.

facilities: 🏃 ♿

Warwick Castle

WARWICK

Warwick Castle, Warwick, CV34 4QU
t: 0870 442 2000   **w:** warwick-castle.co.uk

open:	Jan–Mar, daily 1000–1700. Apr–Sep, daily 1000–1800. Oct–Dec, daily 1000–1700.
admission:	£15.95
description:	Set in 60 acres of grounds with state rooms, armoury, dungeon, torture chamber, 'A Royal Weekend Party 1898', 'Kingmaker' and the new Mill and Engine House.

facilities: ☕ 🏃 ♿

Charlecote Park
(National Trust)

WELLESBOURNE

Charlecote Park (National Trust), Wellesbourne, CV35 9ER
t: (01789) 470277   w: nationaltrust.org.uk

open:	House: Apr–Oct, Mon–Tue, Fri–Sun 1200–1700. Dec, Sat–Sun 1200–1600. Gardens: Mar–Oct, Mon–Tue, Fri–Sun 1030–1800. Nov–Dec, Sat–Sun 1100–1600.
admission:	£7.90
description:	Home of Lucy family since 1247, present house built 1550. Park landscaped by Capability Brown, supports a herd of fallow deer. Tudor gatehouse.
facilities:	💻 🏃 ⛩ ♿

Mary Arden's House
and the Shakespeare Countryside Museum

WILMCOTE

Mary Arden's House and the Shakespeare Countryside
Museum, Wilmcote, CV37 9UN   t: (01789) 293455
w: shakespeare.org.uk

open:	Apr–May, daily 1000–1700. Jun–Aug, daily 0930–1700. Sep–Oct, daily 1000–1700. Nov–Mar, daily 1000–1600.
admission:	£6.00
description:	The childhood home of Shakespeare's mother, and an example of a Tudor farmstead. Also Palmer's Farm, the countryside museum and falconry demonstrations.
facilities:	💻 🏃 ⛩ ♿

Wightwick Manor (National Trust)

WOLVERHAMPTON

Wightwick Manor (National Trust), Wightwick Bank, Wolverhampton, WV6 8EE   **t:** (01902) 761400
w: nationaltrust.org.uk

open:	House: Apr–Dec, Thu–Sat 1230–1700.
	Gardens: Apr–Dec, Wed–Sat 1100–1800.
admission:	£7.50
description:	Begun in 1887, a notable example of William Morris-influenced original wallpapers and fabrics, Kempe glass, de Morgan ware, yew-hedge gardens, pottery studio and William Morris shop.
facilities:	

Arundel Castle

ARUNDEL

Arundel Castle, Arundel, BN18 9AB
t: (01903) 883136   **w:** arundelcastle.org

open:	Mar–Oct, Tue–Sun 1100–1630.
admission:	£6.50
description:	Fortified castle and stately home since 1067. Fine works of art. Medieval keep. Fitzalan chapel. Grounds, kitchen and flower gardens. Special-events programme.
facilities:	

Saint Mary's House and Gardens

St Mary's House and Gardens,
Bramber, BN44 3WE
t: (01903) 816205
w: stmarysbramber.co.uk

open: Apr–Oct, daily 1000–1800.

admission: £6.00

description: A medieval timber-framed Grade I house with rare 16thC wall-leather, fine panelled rooms and a unique painted room. Five acres of beautiful gardens including topiary.

facilities: 🍽 ♿

Goodwood House

Goodwood House, Goodwood, Chichester, PO18 0PX
t: (01243) 755000   **w:** goodwood.co.uk

open: 25 Mar–9 Oct, Sun–Mon 1300–1700. 5–30 Aug, Sun–Thu 1300–1700. Last entry 1600. Closed for occasional event days – phone (01243) 755040 before visiting.

admission: £8.00

description: Goodwood House is the Regency home of the Dukes of Richmond. Collections include significant paintings by George Stubbs and Canaletto, unique Sevres porcelain, fine French furniture and beautiful tapestries.

facilities: 🍽 ♿

Standen

Standen, West Hoathly Road, East Grinstead, RH19 4NE
t: (01342) 323029   **w:** nationaltrust.org.uk

open: Apr–Jul, Wed–Sun 1100–1630.
Aug, Mon, Wed–Sun 1100–1630. Sep–
Oct, Wed–Sun 1100–1630. Nov–Dec,
Mar, Sat–Sun 1100–1500.
admission: £7.50

description: A large family house built in 1894, designed by
Philip Webb, which remains unchanged with
its Morris textiles and wallpapers. Fine views
from the hillside gardens.

facilities:

Uppark

Uppark, South Harting, Petersfield, GU31 5QR
t: (01730) 825857   **w:** nationaltrust.org.uk

open: Apr–Oct, Mon–Thu, Sun 1230–1630.
admission: £7.50

description: Extensive exhibition shows the exciting work
which restored this beautiful house and its
treasures. Rescued paintings, ceramics and
famous dolls' house. Nostalgic servants'
rooms.

facilities:

Petworth House and Park

Petworth House and Park, Petworth, GU28 0AE
t: (01798) 342207   **w:** nationaltrust.org.uk/petworth

open:	House: Apr–Oct, Mon–Wed, Sat–Sun 1100–1700. Park: Daily 0800–dusk.
admission:	£9.00
description:	A late 17thC mansion set in 'Capability' Brown landscaped park. The house is noted for its paintings, Gibbons carvings and fine collection of furniture and sculpture.
facilities:	🍽 ✗ ♿

Stansted Park

Stansted Park, Rowland's Castle, PO9 6DX
t: (023) 9241 2265   **w:** stanstedpark.co.uk

open:	House: Apr–Jun, Mon, Sun 1300–1700. Jul–Aug, Mon–Wed, Sun 1300–1700. Gardens: Daily 0900–1700.
admission:	£6.00

description: A beautiful house with ancient chapel, walled gardens and arboretum surrounded by parkland and forest. The house contains the Bessborough collection of paintings and family furnishings.

facilities: 🍽 ✗ ⛱ ♿

Parham House and Gardens

STORRINGTON

Parham House and Gardens, Parham Park, Storrington, RH20 4HS **t:** (01903) 744888

open:	Apr–Jul, Sep, Wed–Thu, Sun, Bank Hols 1200–1700. Aug, Tue–Fri, Sun, Bank Hols 1200–1700.
admission:	£6.00
description:	An Elizabethan house set in a deer park with great hall, great parlour, saloon and long gallery. Displays include portraits, needlework, tapestries. Also gardens and a maze.

facilities:

Priest House

WEST HOATHLY

Priest House, North Lane, West Hoathly, RH19 4PP
t: (01342) 810479   **w:** sussexpast.co.uk

open:	Mar–Oct, Tue–Sun 1030–1730.
admission:	£2.90

description: Set in the surroundings of a traditional cottage garden, The Priest House is an early 15thC timber-framed hall-house which contains displays of domestic furniture and equipment.

facilities:

Lotherton Hall & Gardens

ABERFORD

Lotherton Hall & Gardens, Aberford, LS25 3EB
t: (0113) 281 3259   w: leeds.gov.uk

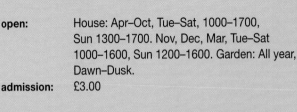

open:	House: Apr–Oct, Tue–Sat, 1000–1700, Sun 1300–1700. Nov, Dec, Mar, Tue–Sat 1000–1600, Sun 1200–1600. Garden: All year, Dawn–Dusk.
admission:	£3.00
description:	Edwardian gentleman's country house with formal Edwardian gardens including abundant herbaceous borders and a wildflower lawn. Paintings, furniture, silver, porcelain, 19thC and 20thC art. Deer park and bird garden.
facilities:	

Oakwell Hall & Country Park

BIRSTALL

Oakwell Hall & Country Park, Nutter Lane, Birstall, WF17 9LG
t: (01924) 326245   w: oakwellhallcountrypark.co.uk

open:	All year, Mon–Fri 1100–1700, Sat–Sun 1200–1700.
admission:	£2.00
description:	This Elizabethan manor house has delighted visitors for centuries. Charlotte Brontë was a regular visitor, and Oakwell Hall featured as Fieldhead, the home of the heroine in Charlotte's novel, Shirley.
facilities:	

Bolling Hall

Bolling Hall, Bowling Hall Road, Bradford, BD4 7LP
t: (01274) 723057   **w:** bradford.gov.uk

open:	All year, Wed–Fri, Bank Hols 1100–1600, Sat 1000–1500, Sun 1200–1500.
description:	Period house, medieval tower to 18thC wing. Period furnishings and splendid oak furniture, central hall with early stained-glass windows.
facilities:	✗ ⌂ ♿

Piece Hall

Piece Hall, Halifax, HX1 1RE
t: (01422) 358087
w: calderdale.gov.uk

open:	All year, Mon–Wed 0800–1800, Thu 0700–1800, Fri 0800–1800, Sat 0700–1800, Sun 0800–1800.
description:	Built in 1779 and restored in 1976, this Grade I Listed building forms a unique and striking monument to the wealth and importance of the wool trade before the industrial revolution.
facilities:	▬ ♘ ⌂ ♿

Shibden Hall

Shibden Hall, Lister's Road, Halifax, HX3 6XG
t: (01422) 352246   w: calderdale.gov.uk

open:	Mar–Nov. Mon–Sat 1000–1700, Sun 1200–1700. Dec–Feb, Mon–Sat 1000–1600, Sun 1200–1600.
admission:	£3.50

description: Dating from c1420, the hall is a distinctive half-timbered building furnished in the styles of the17thC, 18thC and 19thC. An important 17thC aisled barn houses a collection of horse-drawn vehicles.

facilities: ▄ ⚔ ⪥ ♿

Harewood House

Harewood House, Harewood, LS17 9LG
t: (0113) 218 1010   w: harewood.org

open:	Mar–Oct, daily 1000–1600. Winter, please phone for details.
admission:	£12.50

description: The home of the Earl of Harewood is renowned for its stunning architecture and exquisite Adam interiors, and contains a rich collection of Chippendale furniture, fine porcelain and art collections.

facilities: ▄ 🐕 ⪥ ♿

East Riddlesden Hall (NT)

KEIGHLEY

East Riddlesden Hall (National Trust), Bradford Road,
Keighley, BD20 5EL   **t:** (01535) 607075
w: nationaltrust.org.uk

open:	Apr–Jun, Tue–Wed, Sat–Sun 1200–1700.
	Jul–Aug, Mon–Wed, Sat–Sun 1200–1700.
	Sep–Oct, Tue–Wed, Sat–Sun 1200–1700.
admission:	£4.00

description:	A homely 17thC merchant's house with fine plaster ceilings and mullioned windows. The house contains beautiful embroideries, textiles and Yorkshire oak furniture. Delightful garden, shop and tearoom.

facilities: ☕ 🐕 ⛹ ♿

Temple Newsam
House and Farm

LEEDS

Temple Newsam House and Farm, Temple Newsam,
Leeds, LS15 0AD   **t:** (0113) 264 5535
w: leeds.gov.uk/templenewsam

open:	Farm: Winter, Tue–Sun 1000–1600. Summer, Tue–Sun 1000–1700. House: Winter, Tue–Sun 1030–1600, Summer, Tue–Sun 1030–1700.
admission:	£5.50

description:	The farm has over 400 head of stock including cattle, pigs, sheep, goats and poultry. Piglets, hens and cats run free around the farmyard.

facilities: ☕ 🐕 ⛹ ♿

Nostell Priory (NT)

Nostell Priory (National Trust), Doncaster Road, Nostell, WF4 1QE   **t:** (01924) 863892   **w:** nationaltrust.org.uk

open:	Park: All year, daily 0900–1700. House: Apr–Oct. Wed–Sun, 1300–1700. Dec, daily 1200–1600.
admission:	£6.50

description: A Palladian house built in 1733 by James Paine, where Chippendale started his career. The house probably exhibits some of the cabinet maker's finest work.

facilities: 🍽 🐕 🪑 ♿

Pontefract Castle

Pontefract Castle, Castle Chain, Pontefract, WF8 1QH
t: (01977) 723440

open: Apr–Oct, Mon–Fri 0830–1700, Sat–Sun 0930–1815. Nov–Mar, Mon–Fri 0830–dusk, Sat–Sun 1000–1700.

description: In the Middle Ages, Pontefract Castle was one of the most important fortresses in the country. It became a royal castle in 1399, upon the accession of Henry Bolinbroke to the throne.

facilities: 🐕 ♿

Sandal Castle

SANDAL

Sandal Castle, Manygates Lane, Sandal, WF2 7DS
t: (01924) 249779

open:	Apr–Oct, daily 1100–1630. Nov–Mar, Sat–Sun, School Hols 1100–1600.
description:	Sandal Castle stands in a commanding position overlooking the River Calder. Remains of the 13thC stone castle and the fine motte and bailey can be seen on site.
facilities:	🐕 ⛩ ♿

Avebury Manor and Garden

AVEBURY

Avebury Manor and Garden, Avebury, SN8 1RF
t: (01672) 539250

open:	House: Apr–Oct, Mon–Tue, Sun 1400–1640. Garden: Apr–Oct, Mon–Tue, Fri–Sun 1100–1700.
admission:	£4.00
description:	Manorhouse of monastic origins. Present buildings date from early 16thC with Queen Anne alterations and Edwardian renovations. Gardens.
facilities:	🐕 ⛩ ♿

Bowood House and Gardens

Bowood House and Gardens, The Estate Office, Bowood, Calne, SN11 0LZ   **t:** (01249) 812102
w: bowood-house.co.uk

open: Apr–Oct, daily 1100–1730.
admission: £7.70

description: An 18th century house by Robert Adam. Collections of paintings, watercolours, Victoriana and porcelain. Landscaped park with lake, terraces, waterfall and grotto.

facilities: ☕ 🎣 ⛱ ♿

Lacock Abbey

Lacock Abbey, Lacock, SN15 2LG
t: (01249) 730227   **w:** nationaltrust.org.uk

open: Apr–Oct, Mon, Wed–Sun 1300–1730.
admission: £6.30

description: Founded in the 13thC and dissolved in 1539 since when it has been the home of the Talbot family. Medieval cloisters, 18thC Gothic hall and 16thC stable court.

facilities: 🐕 ⛱ ♿

Mompesson House

Mompesson House, The Cathedral Close, Salisbury, SP1 2EL
t: (01722) 335659   **w:** nationaltrust.org.uk

open:	Apr–Oct, Mon–Wed, Sat–Sun 1100–1700.
admission:	£4.40

description: Built c1701 for Charles Mompesson, the house has a graceful staircase and magnificent plasterwork. Collection of English 18thC drinking glasses. Delightful walled garden.

facilities:

Longleat

Longleat, Estate Office, Longleat, Warminster,
BA12 7NW   **t:** (01985) 844400   **w:** longleat.co.uk

open: 17–25 Feb, 31 Mar–4 Nov, daily. 3 Mar–25 Mar, Sat–Sun. See website or phone for opening times and further details.
admission: £10.00

description: Longleat combines the magic of the old with the marvels of the new. From safari park to stately home, mazes to simulator rides. Set in over 9,000 acres of beautiful Wiltshire countryside.

facilities:

Wilton House

Wilton House, The Estate Office, Wilton, SP2 0BJ
t: (01722) 746720   **w:** wiltonhouse.com

open:	House: Apr–Aug, Mon–Fri, Sun, Bank Hols 1030–1730. Garden: Apr–Sep, daily 1030–1730.
admission:	£12.00
description:	Magnificent state rooms, world famous art collection, introductory film, recreated Victorian laundry and Tudor kitchen, landscaped parks, gardens and adventure playground.
facilities:	💻 🐕 🪑 ♿

Witley Court

Witley Court, Great Witley, WR6 6JT
t: (01299) 896636   **w:** english-heritage.org.uk

open:	Apr–May, Sep–Oct, Mar, daily 1000–1700. June–Aug, daily 1000–1700.Nov–Feb, Mon, Thu–Sun 1000–1600.
admission:	£5.20
description:	Spectacular ruins of one of England's great country houses surrounded by magnificent landscaped gardens designed by Nesfield, and featuring the great Perseus and Andromeda fountain.
facilities:	💻 🐕 🪑 ♿

Hanbury Hall
(National Trust)

HANBURY

Hanbury Hall (National Trust), School Road, Hanbury,
WR9 7EA   **t:** (01527) 821214   **w:** nationaltrust.org.uk

open:	Mar–Oct, Mon–Wed, Sat–Sun 1300–1700. Nov–Feb, Sat–Sun 1300–1700.
admission:	£6.80
description:	Beautiful English country house with tranquil 18thC gardens and views over 400 acres of parkland. Unusual features include outstanding murals, mushroom house and bowling green.
facilities:	✕ ⊼ ♿